CONTENTS

KING ARTHUR
AND THE KNIGHTS
OF THE ROUND TABLE

Anne Berthelot

DISCOVERIES®
HARRY N. ABRAMS, INC., PUBLISHERS

12

The history of the British Isles has been a turbulent one with wave after wave of invaders landing on British shores and contending for territorial supremacy. Though fewer in number, the Romans exerted the most lasting influence on Britain during the early Middle Ages – an influence that did much to shape the Arthurian legend.

CHAPTER 1

THE HISTORICAL CONTEXT

Medieval writers had rather fanciful ideas about geography and the kingdom of Logres (scene of the Arthurian legend) bears little real resemblance to the British Isles, depicted (left) around 534. The kingdom of Orkney may perhaps be identified as the Orkney Islands, but the majority of important locations associated with the legend remain a mystery. Right: miniature showing the forts along the Saxon coast in Carolingian times.

Britain under Roman rule in the 5th century

The Romans invaded Britain around 50 BC under Julius Caesar's rule. Despite the fact that Caesar's second campaign ended in a resounding victory, obliging the Ancient Britons to pay tribute to their conquerors (for a few years at least), it is not until the reign of the Emperor Claudius that it is possible to speak of Roman domination of Britain. Even then it was only a partial domination, as is proved by the existence of the Roman 'walls' (Hadrian's Wall, the Antonine Wall built for Antoninus Pius and various fragments whose erection is attributed somewhat uncertainly to Agricola and to Septimus Severus). Even during the period when southern Britain was officially part of the Roman Empire, throughout the region currently known as Scotland, the Scottish and the Picts (so called because of

Unlike Gaul, the British Isles were never really a Roman 'province', the northern-most regions, Scotland and even Northumberland largely escaping Roman dominion. To prevent 'barbarian' incursions from the north, a number of Roman emperors built fortified walls (above, Hadrian's Wall) that spanned the width of the island. Each new wall was erected further south, illustrating the progressive weakening of imperial power.

heir habit of emblazoning their naked bodies with 'war paintings' before going into battle) resisted the invader, frequently provoking bloody encounters.

Generally, the Romans rarely ventured beyond an imaginary line linking the River Tyne and the Solway Firth. As barbarian pressures increased on the limes and the imperial armies were forced to engage with their enemies, so to speak, on their own ground, the distant province of Britain became a secondary preoccupation. From AD 410 it seemed clear that the Romans had relinquished their hold on the island for good.

The Romans had a tradition, however, of extending citizenship to barbarian races recently conquered by Rome and recruiting as many of them as possible to defend the far corners of the Empire. It was in line with this tradition that the final years of the Roman occupation witnessed the installation of Sarmatian legions on the borders of Wales. These soldiers, who had been superficially Romanized, would have imported into Britain their mythology and their heroes, and it is this fact that accounts for some strange similarities between the Arthurian legend and some Sarmatian myths.

The great invasions

The fall of the Roman Empire was caused in the last analysis by the cumulative force of successive invasions: as wave after wave of invaders arrived from the East, even the highly adaptable structures of Roman imperialism eventually crumbled.

As far as Britain was concerned, these invasions were nothing new in themselves. Indeed, as the myths relating to the origins of Ireland suggest, the human race was only the fifth to populate the isles; they were

Like the Greeks, the Romans tended to view foreigners as 'barbarians'. Medieval writers adopted the same attitude with regard to the Picts (below), frequently describing them as related to the Saxon invaders (there is some historical truth in the description) or as the last representatives of a prehuman race, descendants of giants and devils, the earliest inhabitants of Britain.

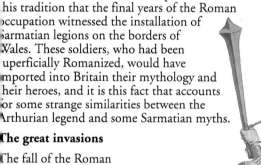

preceded (in third place) by the Fomore, a particularly cruel race of giants, and the Tuatha Dé Danaan (or 'tribes of the Goddess Dana'), who conquered the giants but were in turn expelled by the 'Britons' or 'Gaels' and took refuge in the underground world of the burial mounds or 'sidh' – in other words, in that Other World associated with death and magic. There are traces still of their existence in the folklore of the British Isles, the descendants of the Tuatha Dé Danaan being the 'Little People' (goblins and fairies).

The situation is almost as confusing from a historical perspective. It seems clear that the 'Britons', who belonged to the generic group known as the Celts, did indeed subjugate the original Celtic settlers of the island, but without ultimately succeeding in dominating the northern tribes, who were apparently of Germanic origin. The Picts were never integrated, and with the new waves of invasions that followed in the 4th and 5th centuries they tended to make common cause with the invader. The same was true for the Scottish. When the

We know very little about the religion of the ancient Celts and part of the reason for this is that the Druids (below, an 18th-century engraving of one) appear to have favoured oral rather than written transmission of knowledge. The Druids nevertheless left their mark on the particular form assumed by Christianity in the British Isles – despite the efforts of continental bishops to impose orthodoxy.

Saxons arrived they received a warm welcome north of the Humber, and during their early initiatives were able to launch campaigns in the south and return north to the territory of their allies the Picts and the Scottish in order to find fresh supplies. Further south, Wales, where the Irois (or Irish) rapidly gained a foothold and

The cauldron found at Gundestrup in Denmark (left) is one of the few existing Celtic remains that has a cultural rather than a martial function. This

integrated themselves among the region's earlier settlers, was to be one of the centres of Briton resistance to the Saxon advance and, later, the Norman Conquest.

Who was Arthur?

There was one event that was firmly imprinted in the memories of Ancient Britons and Romans alike – remembered with nostalgia by the one and with horror by the other: the epic story of the usurper Maximus who crossed the Channel at the head of an army and marched on Rome to proclaim himself emperor in AD 383. He died shortly afterwards, but not before he had considerably undermined Roman authority. Maximus swiftly assumed mythic status in the national

gilded silver basin, discovered in Jutland and dating from the 1st century BC, may be one of the prototypes for the Holy Grail. It represents various Celtic deities, in particular the 'Gallic Hercules', a gigantic figure to which several smaller figures are chained, and an antlered god surrounded by wild animals (perhaps the great god of Celtic forests, Cernunnos).

imagination and took his place in the pantheon of
heroes alongside Brennus, the Gallic, that is to say
Celtic, conqueror of Rome.

However, Maximus was not the only Ancient Briton
to sail across the sea and wage war on Gaul; others did
the same, sometimes at the invitation of Gallic chieftains

The Britons eagerly
adopted Roman
civilization, as portrayed
in this 19th-century
painting.

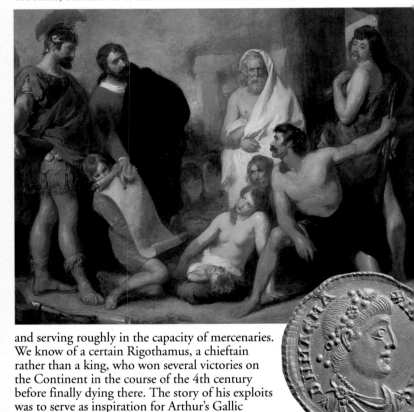

and serving roughly in the capacity of mercenaries.
We know of a certain Rigothamus, a chieftain
rather than a king, who won several victories on
the Continent in the course of the 4th century
before finally dying there. The story of his exploits
was to serve as inspiration for Arthur's Gallic
campaign.

The Saxons did not settle in Britain overnight and
nor was the Roman departure effected in a matter of
months. Not all the old campaigners returned home
when their period of service came to an end: some
settled in Britain, married native women and founded
a family line. We find traces of a kind of Romanized

A Roman coin
showing the bust
of Maximus, or Prince
Macsen, the inspiration
for Arthur's pretensions
to the imperial throne.

aristocracy who endeavoured to keep up Roman traditions, customs and culture and to continue to fight the Saxons and other invaders long after Rome had 'abandoned' them. One of their number, a 'centurion' named Lucius Artorius Castus, may have served as a prototype for Arthur.

Even disregarding the Roman presence, which no doubt persisted well beyond AD 410, it seems clear that the Ancient Britons sought to resist the Pictish, Scottish and Saxon invaders by regrouping so as to create a unified front against them. The socio-political structure of the country, however, does not appear to have favoured the emergence of a supreme commander, still less a king. The Ancient Britons seem to have been divided between a multitude of minor kingdoms ruled by as many petty kings who were more anxious to battle out their differences with immediate neighbours than to unite against a common foe. There are written references, nevertheless, to a period of twenty-odd years at the end of the 5th century when there was a pause in the Saxon advance and the Britons won a series of victories under the leadership of an exceptional general: the texts were undoubtedly referring to Arthur.

The archaeological contribution

Even so, the historical analysis remains a matter of guesswork and Arthur himself has never been precisely identified, nor do we know the extent of his victories or precisely when they occurred. In the hope of confirming their suspicions, historians have turned to archaeology to provide firm evidence, but the conclusions have not been particularly convincing. Archaeological excavations and toponymic studies have provided the possibility of several different

This Anglo-Saxon helmet (below) was reconstructed from a helmet discovered in an Anglo-Saxon tomb at Benty Grange in Derbyshire in 1848. The original dates from the 7th century. It associates a Christian symbol (the cross on the nosepiece) and a pagan symbol (the crest in the form of a boar). In the prophecies attributed to Merlin, Arthur is frequently referred to as the Boar of Cornwall.

Arthurs without enabling us to determine which is the correct one. It is certain, for example, that the name Caerleon (one of Arthur's capitals) comes from Castra Legionum, which is associated today with Chester. The problem with this argument is that there were undoubtedly several Castra Legionum at the time of the Roman occupation.

A relatively high proportion of place names prominently cited in the first literary texts associated with the Arthurian legend can in fact be identified. A map of the significant locations of the Arthurian legend can be drawn and links Cornwall (Tintagel, Arthur's birthplace), Salisbury Plain (Stonehenge, monument to Pendragon) and the ancient regions of 'East Anglia' and 'West Anglia' (named after the Angles, those marauding companions of the Saxons). But is Cadbury Castle Camelot? Traces of fortifications have been found at Cadbury that indicate the presence of a military structure and castle in approximately the 5th century, but is this sufficient to link the site conclusively with Arthur? Badon Hill, north of Salisbury, could be the site of the key battle of Mount Badon, thanks to which the Saxon advance was halted for almost half a century, but again we cannot be certain.

The stone circle at Stonehenge (below) on Salisbury Plain is one of the great mysteries of the Neolithic age. It was almost certainly an astronomical and religious complex where the movement of the stars could be observed and plotted according to sophisticated calculations, which in turn probably determined the course of liturgical rites of which we know nothing today. From its earliest mention in the Arthurian legend Stonehenge was associated with the monument erected by Merlin in memory of Pendragon, brother of Uther Pendragon, Arthur's father.

The matter is further complicated by the fact that a number of historians, basing their theories on what we know of the political situation in the 5th and 6th centuries, suggest that during Arthur's (presumed) lifetime the Saxons had not advanced so far south and that the decisive battles, in particular the Battle of Camlann when the king supposedly lost his life, must

The ruins of Tintagel (above), the Duke of Cornwall's impregnable fortress, where he shut up his wife Igraine to protect her from the advances of Uther Pendragon.

The Arthurian legend and Celtic landmarks

It was in the 16th century that the antiquarian John Leland first identified Cadbury Castle (opposite below) with Camelot, Arthur's legendary capital. Recent archaeological excavations at the site confirm the presence of fortifications dating from the probable time of the 'historical' Arthur, in other words the 5th–6th centuries. Arthur's birthplace, Tintagel (this page, above), sits high above the sea at the far tip of the Cornish peninsula. Stonehenge (this page, below) has also been assimilated into the Arthurian legend, since Merlin is supposed to have brought the 'giants' stones' over from Ireland by magic and erected the site as a monument to Pendragon. Near Castle Dore in Cornwall there is a standing stone (opposite right) inscribed with the words 'Drustanus, son of Cunomor'. Drustanus is the Latin version of Tristan, another figure assimilated by the legend in the 13th century as one of the Knights of the Round Table. Maiden Castle in Dorset (opposite above) was another castle in the kingdom of Logres.

The Christianization of the sites

The 13th-century texts emphasized the resemblance between Arthur and Charlemagne by repeatedly referring to Arthur as a Christian king leading a veritable crusade against the (pagan) Saxon invaders. At the time of the historical Arthur matters were almost certainly not so clear-cut. Christianity was slow to take a hold in England. Its introduction was effected in particular by missionaries from Ireland, to whose influence this 9th-century cross at Islay in Scotland (left) is a clear testimony. Churches and abbeys were often built on ancient sites associated with pagan worship, as was the case at Old Sarum in Wiltshire (left), one of the oldest Christian sites in southern Britain.

have taken place only a short distance from Hadrian's Wall, on the border with Scotland. They present a plausible case for quite a different site for Camlann and Camelot, as well as etymological arguments that are just as convincing as those argued by proponents of the southern hypothesis.

In the 12th century the debate was widened – for reasons of political propaganda – by the monks of Glastonbury Abbey, who sought to reconstruct the scene

Below: Ordnance Survey plan of Cadbury Castle, which is situated on the River Camel and dates from the 5th century. The fortifications are built on a site that was already virtually impregnable. Local place names, such as 'Arthur's Well' (which

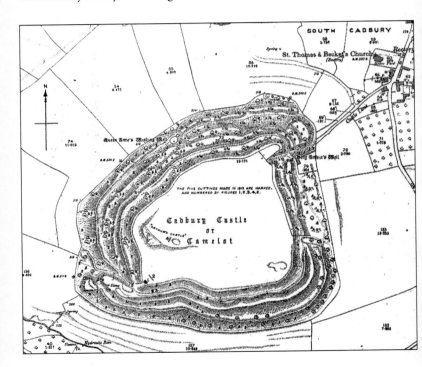

of the legend with the abbey at its centre. Drawing on and, where need be, simply correcting and modifying the evidence contained in earlier texts (which was in any case vague), the monks at Glastonbury succeeded in drawing up a map of the Arthurian legend that extended from Cornwall to Wales and included Salisbury, Winchester and the Thames Valley.

is supposed to have magical powers), show an association with the legend. Camaalot in the French texts became Camelot in the English and the name has been retained in this form.

The earliest literary texts and representations

Arthur's name is mentioned in the texts from a very early date, and yet there is still a gap of at least eighty or a hundred years between the events described and the chronicles recording them.

The oldest text is Gildas' *De excidio Britanniae* (On the Downfall of Britain), written in around AD 550, less than a century after the events themselves had unfolded. It is even possible that the author may have gleaned certain details from first-hand evidence. But Gildas was a 'saint' and his account is vehemently partisan, reorganizing the historical truth to fit the theory he is seeking to demonstrate: that

Above: detail of a map of Britain (1715), showing Wales and the West Country. In support of its long tradition of independence, Wales lays claim to numerous locations associated with the Arthurian legend, and in particular with Merlin, Merlinus Ambrosius, the prophet and magician whose birthplace is Carmarthen (Caer Myrddin, 'town of Merlin').

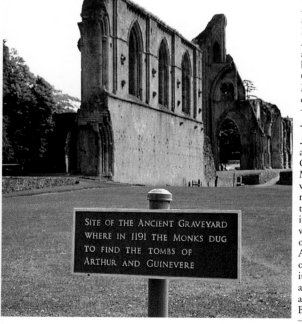

SITE OF THE ANCIENT GRAVEYARD WHERE IN 1191 THE MONKS DUG TO FIND THE TOMBS OF ARTHUR AND GUINEVERE

Left: reputed site of the tomb of Arthur and Guinevere at Glastonbury. In the Middle Ages the town was surrounded by marshland and it is to this watery location that it owes its identification with the 'Isle of Glass' of the ancient Celts. An important place of pagan worship, it became, with the advent of Christianity, a natural place for a Benedictine abbey.

Britain had embarked on an irremediable process of destruction thanks to the dissolution of its moral values. While giving due weight to Arthur's battles and victories against the pagan enemy, he also presents the picture of a secular sovereign who comes repeatedly into conflict with the men of God – which inevitably brings about his downfall.

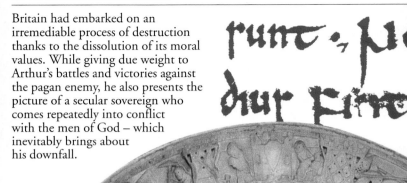

The *Annales Cambriae* (Annals of Cambria) designed post-956 to catalogue year by year, like all annals, the significant events of a period, in fact tell us very little. There was a chieftain, or king, they say, by the name of Arthur, who won twelve victories, essentially thanks to his Christian faith, the visible sign of which he carried with him in the form of an image of the Virgin Mary painted on the inside of his shield. His victory at the pivotal battle of Mount Badon, moreover, was due to the fact that he had done penance for twenty-four hours prior to the conflict by reproducing the stages of Christ's Passion.

Formerly attributed to the chronicler known as Nennius, the *Historia Britonum* (The History of the Britons) is now considered to be an anonymous text. It is possible that an earlier version of the chronicle existed at the beginning of the 9th century, with a *terminus ante quem* of AD 801. It was this chronicle that gave perhaps

Above: archivolt in Modena Cathedral depicting the abduction of a female figure by knights. Three names are inscribed in the stone: 'Art[hur]', 'Guen[evere]' and 'Melw[a]s', Melvas (or Meleagant, as he is known in the 12th-century romances of Chrétien de Troyes), the knight who carried off Arthur's queen. This piece of sculpture is one of the earliest examples of the wide circulation of the Arthurian legend beyond the Celtic world.

*arturur & echo
on longo port tr̃*

the clearest picture of Arthur before Geoffrey of
Monmouth's decisive work, and no doubt Geoffrey
of Monmouth derived much of his information from
the earlier work. Less fanciful than Gildas' text, and
more complete than the *De excidio*, the *Historia
Britonum* devotes a chapter to enumerating Arthur's
twelve battles, concentrating in particular on the
last, the great and tragic Battle of Camlann.

It was in a 7th-century
Latin manuscript,
the *Life of Saint
Columbanus*, that the
name of King Arthur
was first mentioned.
Above: the first line
of the manuscript.

Left: a mosaic in the
cathedral at Otranto,
Sicily, showing Arthur –
the name *Rex Arturus* is
clearly legible to the
right of the figure –
mounted on what looks
like a goat and doing
battle with a monstrous
cat. This appears to be
an ancient motif drawn
from folklore and
having no connection
with the historical
versions of the legend.

HENRY. II

Though it went on to develop in unexpected directions, the Arthurian legend had its beginnings in political pragmatism and was largely the creation of the Angevin dynasty – a means of establishing its authority and outmanoeuvring its rivals. While the Capetians claimed their descent from Charlemagne, the Plantagenets countered with the story of King Arthur and the Round Table.

CHAPTER 2

THE CREATION OF A LEGEND

Left: Henry Plantagenet, crowned King of England in 1154. He was a man of culture, who understood how literature – for example, Merlin's famous prophecies in Geoffrey of Monmouth's *Historia regum Britanniae* – could be used as propaganda. Right: Merlin building Stonehenge.

The Battle of Hastings and the Norman invasion

VBI hAROLD

In 1066, following a series of confusing dynastic disputes, William the Conqueror led an army across the Channel and landed at Hastings, where he defeated the English under King Harold. William was crowned in his stead and Britain once more faced the vagaries of life under an occupying force. The effects of this new invasion, however, were not so much military as cultural and economic. The Normans under William were descended from those same 'Men of the North' (as the Vikings were known) who settled Normandy by force before their leader Rollo finally agreed to pay

This page and opposite: words and images from the Bayeux Tapestry, or Queen Matilda's Tapestry, as it is also known. The tapestry, thought have been made at the time of the Norman Conquest of England i the 11th century, is an

tribute to the King of France for the privilege of occupying the region. For the past century, however, the Normans had come under the civilizing influence of the Roman provinces with their more advanced customs and manners. Their language in particular bore the evidence of this successful assimilation, since they spoke a 'Romance' dialect, Anglo-Norman, which was to become the language of the court and of the nobility, the language of literature and propaganda.

embroidered linen stri about 70 metres long which records in pictures the various historical events leadin up to the Battle of Hastings and the victo of William the Bastard Duke of Normandy (later known as Willia the Conqueror).

CRAMENTVM·FECIT·
LELMO DVCI:

Relations were strained between the Norman invaders nd those earlier arrivals, the Saxons, who now found themselves confronted with the gentlest of colonizing measures. The Normans constituted a minority, moreover, and

The famous tapestry describes, among other things, the stormy negotiations which took place between Edward the Confessor, King of

heir position in Britain was not particularly secure. The ghts of the Angevins, Geoffrey Plantagenet and later is son Henry II, needed consolidating, and Geoffrey hrewdly sought support for his position in the history f this country he was determined to rule.

he Angevin dynasty seeks a legitimate role

f it was impossible to disguise the fact that the Vormans were newcomers to Britain, there was evertheless an advantage to be gained from legitimizing he position of the indigenous inhabitants of the ountry – the Britons – by providing them with llustrious origins that linked this relatively remote rritory with the Continent. And in the 12th century ese origins had to be Roman, or Greek, and capable of

England, and the two pretenders to the throne, the Norman William – later William the Conqueror (shown above) – and the Anglo-Saxon Harold, whom the king reputedly designated his successor before Harold's death in 1066. Harold's claim to the throne was disputed by William the Conqueror, who eventually defeated him at the Battle of Hastings.

The influence of the Arthurian legend filtered through into the political domain in sometimes unexpected ways. This miniature (left), representing Arthur and his 'thirty kingdoms', is taken from Pierre de Langtoft *Chronicle*, a 14th-century manuscript which lists France (unexceptionally), but also Albania (Scotland), Norway, Germany and even Rome, Greece and Babylon, among the thirty kingdoms that reputedly paid tribute to the king. The manuscript thus reflects the traditional nostalgia for an *imperium mundi* whereby a Christian sovereign would exercise authority over all the known parts of the world.

establishing a connection between the heroes of Antiquity and the Christian or pre-Christian princes responsible for civilizing 'Britain'. The fact that the cultural heritage of the 'clerics' (the intellectuals of the time) passed through a Christian filter was an irrelevance: since the only culture that existed was Latin, and therefore ecclesiastical, the influence of Antiquity and paganism remained paramount. By a process known as *translatio studii* learning and knowledge were passed from Greece to Rome at the time of Virgil and

ugustus, and henceforth to the West, where the clergy
took it upon themselves to record this precious
inheritance.

The *Historia regum Britanniae*

In 1138 Geoffrey of Monmouth, a member of Geoffrey
Plantagenet's entourage, composed a seminal work
entitled the *Historia regum Britanniae* (The History of
the Kings of Britain). It was a chronicle, in the medieval
sense of the term, in other words a historical text
recording all the major events that had occurred in
Britain since its earliest (mythical) origins.

Having set the scene, the *Historia regum Britanniae*
then moves on to more serious matters, describing the
arrival of the first settlers to bring a civilizing influence
to Britain – the Romans. After a journey strangely
reminiscent of the voyage made
by Aeneas, one of the latter's
descendants, Brutus (or Brute)
arrives on the island's virgin
shores with a small group of
companions following his exile
from Rome as a criminal. The
ship carrying Brutus and his
companions was swept by
chance on to its unknown
shores. The island was at the
time called Albion and was
inhabited by a race of giants,
who were driven into the
mountains. Brutus renames the
island 'Britain' and his companions Britons after himself and
goes on to lay the foundations
for the country's future social
and political structure.

The *Historia regum
Britanniae* then enumerates the
successive kings who ruled over
Britain, the most admirable
among them – and the one to
whom the Latin text devotes the
most space – being King Arthur.

Geoffrey of Monmouth was the first author to collect together the few scattered pieces of evidence relating to Arthur and to build out of them a major myth. Not only did the story of Arthur, elevated to the same status as the great conquerors of the West, provide the Anglo-Norman sovereigns with a reference point and a worthy model; Geoffrey also used Merlin's prophecies to establish a link between the reign of Arthur and the period in which he himself was writing. The enigmatic soothsayer emphasizes the common interest shared by Normans and Britons, who face the same, and implacable, foe – the Saxons – and demonstrates how Britain's future hopes are indissolubly linked to the Norman cause.

Left: Henry II's seal. Below: Eleanor of Aquitaine's tomb. As granddaughter of the first troubadour, Guillaume IX of Aquitaine or Poitiers, Eleanor was responsible for introducing into northern France, and later transplanting to the Anglo-Norman court, the courtly culture evolved in the south. She was one of the most important literary patrons of the second half of the 12th century. Her daughter, Marie de Champagne, the protector of Chrétien de Troyes, is said to have commissioned *Le Chevalier de la charrette*, the first novel to describe the love triangle between Arthur, Guinevere and Lancelot.

Arthur against Charlemagne: Henry Plantagenet's shrewd ploy

When Henry II was crowned King of England in 1154, he was quick to assess the political advantage to be gained from Geoffrey's work. Henry II had two problems on his hands. First, he was involved in a bitter rivalry with the King of France and desperately needed to find a way of legitimizing his rights in France. Second, he needed the support of the Britons against the Saxons, who, even ninety years on, continued to balk at Norman rule.

Henry II was King of England, but he was also Count of Anjou and a vassal of Louis VII, King of France – and, since the first count, the semi-mythical Rollo, the Counts of Anjou had given their allegiance to the King of France. This situation was further complicated by the fact that Henry II had married the recently divorced wife of Louis VII, Eleanor of Aquitaine, and so acquired the duchy of Aquitaine as a dowry settlement – for which he also had to pay

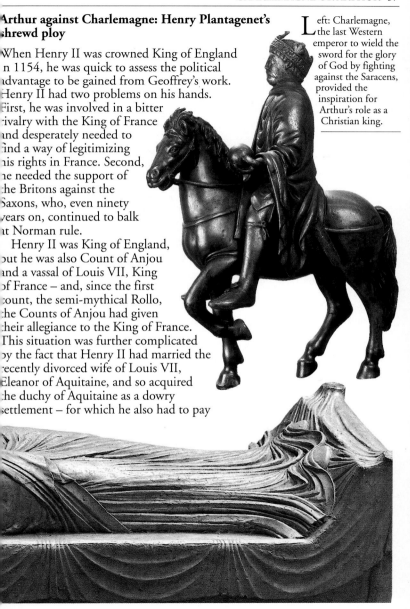

Left: Charlemagne, the last Western emperor to wield the sword for the glory of God by fighting against the Saracens, provided the inspiration for Arthur's role as a Christian king.

homage to the French king. It was vitally important for Henry II that he find a way of shoring up his position and establishing his undisputed royal authority vis-à-vis a rival who enjoyed the prestige of descending from the Frankish emperor Charlemagne, regarded in the 12th century as the forefather of the Capetian kings.

The 'Breton hope'

At home in Britain Henry II was to practise the oft-adopted policy of divide and rule. Rather than attempt to unite the different factions of a kingdom split by dissensions and quarrels, he recognized the advantage to be gained by having the Normans as newcomers to the scene.

And yet the Britons, despite their hatred of the Saxons, were slow to rally to the Plantagenet banner. Their half-heartedness can be explained in part by the fact that written into the Arthurian legend was the belief that the king would one day return in the role of a messiah. Arthur was not dead, the story went: after the Battle of Camlann he had been taken by Morgan le Fay to the island of Avalon so that she could tend his wounds, and he would return to lead his people to victory when the time was right. This was the 'Breton hope', derided

Left: statue of Arthur after a drawing by Dürer, in the Royal Chapel, Innsbruck. Its presence here indicates the widespread popularity of the legend.

by contemporary Latin chroniclers, but apparently representing a sufficiently widespread belief among the Britons themselves to constitute an obstacle to the political ambitions of Henry II.

The first novel: Wace's *Roman de Brut*

The Plantagenet king therefore adopted a twofold strategy. He sought, on the one hand, to turn the legend

Lamentation of King Arthur by William Bell Scott. Arthur's departure for the mysterious isle of Avalon was a favourite theme with the Pre-Raphaelites.

to his own advantage by presenting himself as King Arthur's legitimate heir, while simultaneously putting an end once and for all to the 'Breton hope' and satisfying them with the existence of a real Norman king, who had their interests at heart, rather than a figure of myth. To this end (and with political rather than literary notions in mind) Henry commissioned an Anglo-Norman cleric at his court by the name of Wace to turn the *Historia regum Britanniae* into a novel. What this meant in practice was the translation of the Latin text into the vernacular, that 'Romance' language which was beginning to engender a new type of literature accessible to a public that extended well beyond the confines of monastery walls.

Wace's *Brut* reproduced the events described in the *Historia*, and the basic elements of the legend, which were to resurface throughout the Arthurian literature, found their definitive form here.

Alongside Arthur a handful of other key figures are mentioned, including Sir Kay, Arthur's seneschal or household manager, and Gawain, the king's nephew. The Round Table was an invention of Wace's and corresponded nicely to the twelve Peers who formed Charlemagne's entourage. One of Wace's other innovations, though apparently slight, was to open the way for all the fantastic, or fictional, literature of the 12th and 13th centuries. In Wace's *Brut* Arthur is still the warrior king, the unconquered hero who delivers Britain from the Saxon threat, then goes to the Continent to carve out for himself a kingdom capable of rivalling the Roman Empire; but this is epic material. Wace opens up a new novelistic vein by mentioning that after the decisive battle against the Saxons, and before he went over to the Continent, Arthur presided over twelve years of peace in Britain – a time of adventures and marvels. These were no longer conquests and wars, but stories of individual exploits that borrow heavily from Celtic mythology and allow the novelist's imagination a completely free rein.

From Avalon to Glastonbury

The *Brut* concludes the story of Arthur with the description of his removal to Avalon to await his

Arthur *rex otiosus* (the idle king) took no part in the individual quests of his knights and his oldest characteristic as a warrior chieftain is obscured in the 13th-century romances, where he appears as the symbol of royal power rather than as a person in his own right. This shift in emphasis is not yet apparent in the 12th-century texts, in particular Wace's *Roman de Brut*, where Arthur not only leads his army to victory against France and further afield, in an attempt to overcome Roman authority, but also fights the giant of Mont-Saint-Michel (opposite, miniature) in single combat after the latter has carried off the daughter of his vassal the Duke of Brittany. (She, in turn, was to give her name to the tiny island of Tombelaine, where she is buried.) Battles with giants are a classic theme of narrative literature – the famous Breton stories – and probably derive from a motif of ancient folklore which somehow attached itself to the figure of Arthur the strategist and warrior.

e pres du fn suv le nuure sedit
n gut soit pres la fn turnoit

rthur le guidast ainz euspvendre
uiy gil soit ca maleuis prendre
ais li Geaut arthur choise

ultimate return. However, to satisfy Henry's 'political' needs, the author introduces a double note of uncertainty. What, or where, is the isle of Avalon? And assuming that Arthur has been taken to Avalon by healing fairies, can we be sure that he remained there? As regards the identification of the island, the monks of Glastonbury Abbey, close to Wales, were happy to oblige Henry with a location. The abbey, recently destroyed by fire, was not particularly prosperous, and the monks were no doubt quick to recognize the advantage to be gained from this connection with the mythical isle. The identification of Avalon and Glastonbury was confirmed, moreover, by etymological studies, which were a medieval passion. A Celtic name

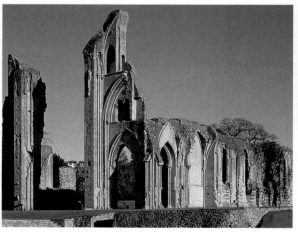

with which Avalon was associated was Ynys-witrin, meaning the 'Isle of Glass'.

The 'Breton hope', for its part, was seriously undermined by a rumour that the fairies had tried in vain to heal the wounded king and after three days had transported the body of the dead Arthur to the shores of Avalon. This new version did nothing to detract from the legend as a whole and, what was more, it dovetailed neatly with Henry's political aims.

The name of Henry II is so closely linked with the story of Arthur that in the 13th century it was generally accepted that Henry had commissioned the entire *Lancelot-Graal* cycle. The text is attributed to

Walter Map, a copyist at the Anglo-Norman court during Henry's reign. In fact, both had been dead for almost fifty years when the texts in question were composed. This early-14th-century miniature (above) represents Henry and Walter in the classic attitude of the patron and his scribe (or the Holy Ghost and one of the Apostles). Above left: the ruins of Glastonbury Abbey.

Henry died in 1189. Shortly after his death the monks of Glastonbury Abbey put the final touches to the revised version of the myth by 'discovering' the tomb of Arthur and Guinevere in the cemetery attached to the abbey. It is not clear whether this piece of theatre had been planned with Henry's knowledge: what we do know is that the king had done much to further the abbey's fortunes during the final years of his reign. The discovery of the two skeletons (Guinevere's still crowned with a magnificent head of golden hair) did not merely deal a fatal blow to the 'Breton hope'; it also guaranteed the authenticity of the legend and turned Arthur into a figure of undeniable historical reality, at the same time enabling those who had played such an important role in his 'invention' – the Plantagenets – to bask in his reflected glory.

A monk at the Benedictine abbey at Glastonbury (then in partial ruins) is reputed to have dreamt of the precise location of Arthur's tomb in the abbey grounds. He is said to have persuaded his brother monks to unearth the body, which was duly identified by a Latin inscription on a cross that subsequently disappeared. The scene is represented in this fanciful work (below) by John Hamilton Mortimer.

Using the scanty details available, the romances constructed an entire biography of King Arthur. Beginning with his conception – assisted by Merlin's magic – they take us through to his death, or removal to the Blessed Isles, a place from which it was said he would one day return to liberate Britain from the invaders' yoke.

CHAPTER 3

THE LIFE OF ARTHUR

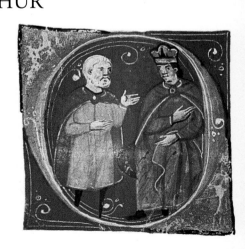

Elected by God, Arthur is crowned king at the age of fifteen (opposite, 15th-century miniature), but rejected as a sovereign on account of his youth and his illegitimacy. Right: 14th-century miniature showing Merlin and Arthur.

The circumstances surrounding Arthur's birth

Like all great heroes, Arthur was born in exceptional circumstances. One of the marks of divine election has always been an unusual birth, in which a god or, in the Christian context, the hand of Providence is seen to play a part. Arthur was the son of the (legendary) king Uther Pendragon and Igraine (or Igerna), the wife of his vassal the Duke of Cornwall.

Thanks to the magical – one might say diabolical – intervention of Merlin, the magician and prophet, Uther was able to assume the guise of the duke and make love to Igraine, who remained unaware of the deception. It was through this ploy that Arthur was conceived, and on the same night the Duke of Cornwall lost his life in a skirmish. Uther later married Igraine (the other version of whose name, Igerna, is an anagram of the Latin for 'queen', *regina*).

According to Celtic tradition, a king must first conquer sovereignty before he can be considered a king. Sovereignty, personified as an old woman who regains her youth in the arms of the would-be king, is the true guarantor of his power. Igraine, conquered by Uther thanks to Merlin's intervention, is clearly a literary embodiment of the principle of sovereignty. Above (on the right): Igraine and Uther Pendragon.

While the older texts (up until the *Roman de Brut*) refer to Arthur as Uther's legitimate heir, the later ones describe him as a bastard, conceived prior to his parents' marriage, and therefore unworthy to become king. This new development was not only a product of the growing unease felt by the aristocracy with regard to contested birthrights and cases of illegitimacy: it also fulfilled the aim of enriching the story by providing the young Arthur with the opportunity to prove his merit to the world by triumphing over adversity. Norman influence created a serious legal problem from the 12th century onwards by contradicting the Celtic law whereby bastards – as long as they were not disowned by their parents – had the same rights as children born in wedlock.

It was for this reason that the original version of the legend was modified in the 12th century along the lines of a classical fairy tale. Since the child the queen is carrying cannot reasonably be regarded as belonging to the king, she is obliged to abandon the baby at birth. The young Arthur is handed into Merlin's care – in payment for his services – and the magician takes it upon himself to have the child educated as a knight by a minor nobleman loyal to the king, whose wife weans

Merlin, the prophet who in Geoffrey of Monmouth tells the usurper Vortigern of his imminent destruction, becomes in the romances a magician capable of all manner of miracles. Personal adviser to King Uther (seen with him, below, in this 14th-century miniature), he also figures alongside the young Arthur during his conflict with the rebel barons, disappearing from the story when he is betrayed by the Lady of the Lake, sometimes called Viviane.

her own child in order to nurse the unknown baby. No one – not even Arthur himself – knows the young boy's true identity.

A 13th-century miniature showing Arthur drawing the

The sword in the stone

In such circumstances, the transfer of power could hardly be automatic, as was the case in the oldest versions of the legend. Uther Pendragon's death deprived Britain of a legitimate sovereign, since Arthur was his only son. Arthur's accession to the throne was to demonstrate in the most striking fashion his status as a divinely elected king, but was also to provoke violent

sword out of the stone and being proclaimed king. Since the sword was a miracle sent by God as a means of designating the rightful king, it was the Archbishop of London who supervised the proceedings of the 'election'.

opposition among high-ranking noblemen.

When the country's great vassals assembled to elect a new sovereign, they were advised by the Archbishop of London to wait for a sign from God. At the end of Mass, on the square in front of the cathedral, they discovered a sword stuck fast in an anvil, itself set into a stone step. An inscription told how only the rightful king would be able to draw the sword from the stone. Each of the barons and knights present tried their luck in turn, but each in turn failed. Then, after a rather fanciful combination of circumstances, Arthur seized the sword and effortlessly drew it out of the stone.

As one might have expected, however, the barons refused to recognize the authority of this unknown youth, despite the unconditional support he received from the archbishop (and through him the Church, which, at the time when these stories were written, was a political force to be reckoned with). The coronation of the new king was delayed, first until

A bove: manuscript representation of the sword in the stone. Below: Arthur's sword, Caledwlch in Celtic tradition, later called Excalibur, was not the sword drawn from the stone, but a sword from the Other World that was given or lent to him by the mysterious Lady of the Lake.

Easter, then until Whitsun. During the intervening period, the barons set about putting young Arthur to the test, but were obliged to bow to his precocious wisdom and innate nobility. Finally Merlin intervened and revealed the truth about Arthur's royal parentage. The revelation failed, however, to win over the barons, who refused to pledge obedience to a bastard. Arthur was crowned by the archbishop. Supported by the common people, who had instantly adopted his cause, and by the poor knights to whom he had promised land and wealth, he nevertheless faced insurrection from the barons. They rallied behind the 'kings' of Orkney and Norgales, who were married to Arthur's half-sisters.

Modred, child of an incestuous relationship

The motif of unknown identity plays a significant part in Arthur's story before we even reach the complicated narrative of the battles. While the barons are waiting in London for the king to be elected, Arthur, the young squire, who has accompanied his adoptive father and brother (both knights and therefore, at least in theory, eligible for election), meets a beautiful woman, the wife of King Lot of Orkney, and falls in love with her. Unwittingly replicating the pattern of events established by his father, he deceives the queen into taking him into her bed, and fathers a son.

This rather banal story of adultery proves, however, to entail, in the medieval view of things, one of the worst

The conflict between Arthur (above, his coronation) and his barons reflects the tensions inherent in feudal society, where the king was only a lord who was marginally more powerful than his neighbours. It appears that at the time of the 'historical' Arthur the Britons were divided into numerous petty kingdoms, which joined forces for the duration of a campaign against the invader, and that Arthur was no more than the 'general' in charge of these campaigns, the *comes bellorum*.

of all possible sins – the sin of incest. The Queen of Orkney is in fact Arthur's half-sister, and the child of this liaison, Modred (or Mordred), will be responsible for his father's death, and for the destruction of his kingdom and of the Arthurian dream. The fault is sometimes attributed to Arthur, sometimes to his sister, depending on the version of the legend: in several texts it is said that the Queen of Orkney, like her sister Morgan, is fully aware of the blood relationship that exists between the two lovers and that she seduces Arthur deliberately, with the intention of bringing about his long-term ruin. This view of things has the

Gawain was the eldest son of Lot of Orkney, and scarcely any younger than his 'uncle' Arthur. He appears early on in the legend as an independent hero with the characteristics of a solar divinity (his strength grows and wanes with the sun). Below: Gawain saving his mother from the Saxons.

advantage of minimizing Arthur's guilt, since the legend requires that he should appear as irreproachable as possible. The truth comes to light when Arthur's lineage is revealed, so that, from the outset of his reign, the king is fully aware of the curse weighing upon him.

From war to peace: Queen Guinevere

While the barons were needlessly waging war on their rightful king – without much success, thanks to Merlin's intervention – the Saxons, who were always quick to profit from any opportunity, succeeded in entering the kingdom and causing considerable havoc. It did not take the rebel barons long to realize that they would be courting disaster unless they made peace with the young king, who, in the interim, had proved himself an astute general and a knight of unrivalled courage and skill. Their cause was in any case weakened by the defection of their sons, who were also in a number of cases Arthur's nephews, and who had sided with their new sovereign. Following a complicated sequence of events, recorded in a series of lengthy narratives in the epic style, the barons acknowledged Arthur as their rightful king (they were never to rebel against his authority again) and with his help succeeded in permanently crushing the Saxon force.

It was during these turbulent times that Arthur, following Merlin's advice, offered his support to the King of Carmelide (a neighbouring kingdom which

Guinevere (left in a 19th-century painting) derives from the Welsh Gwenhwyfar, meaning 'white ghost': it is a name of ill omen, anticipating the negative role Guinevere will later play. In the meantime a paragon of courtly virtue, she renders Arthur an inestimable service by attaching Lancelot, 'the best knight in the world', to the court.

probably paid tribute to the kingdom of Logres), whose people were suffering the onslaught of pagan 'giants' and, for good measure, the Saxons too. This king had a beautiful and accomplished daughter called Guinevere, and when peace was finally concluded, Arthur took her as his wife – despite Merlin's warnings that the queen would betray her husband with his best knight.

The marriage brought to a close a period of military engagements, and ushered in an era of peace and prosperity. A warring king, image of the tribal chieftain ennobled by the Roman designation *comes Britanniae* (overseer of the Britons) could manage without a wife; but a king whose purpose was to act in the manner of a civilizing hero and to found a dynasty needed a queen. Arthur's marriage to Guinevere was the final sign confirming his legitimacy as sovereign.

While Arthur (modelled on Charlemagne) is represented as a man of mature years, sometimes even as an old man, Guinevere is always depicted as a young woman of great beauty. Above: Arthur with Guinevere and his advisers.

Arthur's reign

This was the start of the twelve years of peace referred to in Wace's *Roman de Brut*. It is during this period – which the stories, particularly the 13th-century romances, present as virtually limitless – that the adventures of the Knights of the Round Table occur, and that the revolutionary ideological system of courtly virtues is set in place. From now on, Arthur is no longer a warring king, but a civilizing influence. The repetitive themes of the *chansons de geste* have no further place in his story: there are literally no more enemies to conquer. The Saxons have been pacified, and if the later literary texts set about re-creating an atmosphere of war and conflict by inventing new challenges for Arthur to overcome, his reign is essentially characterized by the display of knightly prowess and by the adventures of individual knights.

When Arthur ceases to be a leader of armies and becomes instead the sovereign of a kingdom enjoying an era of peace, he ceases to be the central hero of the stories that revolve around him. Settled at Camelot, the castle he built to symbolize his power, he remains from now on a shadowy figure. It was not until the end of the

Above: in the earliest texts Arthur's court respects Roman customs in that only the men are present at table. Later the presence of the queen is mentioned. On major festive occasions the king can only begin eating once an adventure takes place: a young woman's request for help or a knight's challenge – any event that confirms the knightly vocation of the Arthurian world.

Middle Ages, when the romantic imagination was unning out of steam and looking for ways to renew tself, that we see him once more occupying the role of a hero in a literary text.

Below: Arthur and his knights returning to Camelot.

The Knights of the Round Table

The king is surrounded by a number of key figures who reappear from one story to the next: Kay, the seneschal (present from the beginning), Bedivere, his cupbearer, Gawain, Agravain, Gaheris and Gareth, his nephews, and Sagramor the Wild; later, Lancelot of the Lake, Guinevere's lover and for a long time the undefeated champion of the realm; Perceval, who goes in search of the Holy Grail; Tristan, nephew of King Mark, and Bohort, Lionel and Lamorat; and finally Galahad, Lancelot's son, the perfect knight, and the traitor Modred, who is the son of Arthur.

All these knights belong to the Round Table, an elite body, whose members take their place at assemblies and banquets at a table that is circular in shape in order to avoid notions of hierarchy and potential conflicts.

The Round Table has a variable number of places: sometimes twelve, sometimes fifty – the upper limit in a realistic representation of the facts – but also one hundred and fifty when Arthur's entourage grows and a maximum number of individuals are to be given the honour of participating.

The Knights of the Round Table are a fellowship bound together by an indissoluble bond: the tragedy of the final battle is also in part the breakdown of this bond. In memory of Judas, there is one seat at the table

Above: Galahad, son of Lancelot and future hero of the Grail, is led to the Knights of the Round Table.

Originally intended to represent the order of the cosmos, the Round Table (left) became merely a token symbol in the later stories before assuming a metaphysical significance once more through the Grail legend. According to the latter, the Round Table was founded by Merlin in memory of the table at which Christ and his twelve Apostles sat together for the Last Supper. It also recalled the table which Joseph of Arimathea devised as a means of distinguishing (thanks to the Grail) the elect from the morally unworthy during the long journey he and his companions made from Jerusalem to England. In the earliest version of the story the Perilous Seat was probably an adaptation of the Lia Fail, or stone of sovereignty in Ireland, which was said to cry out when the new sovereign placed his foot on it. Perceval, who succeeds in claiming the Perilous Seat at his second attempt, not only has access to the spiritual mysteries of the Grail; he also becomes king in place of his uncle, the Fisher King or keeper of the Grail.

which remains permanently vacant: the Perilous Seat. Only the hero of the Grail quest, that is to say, the best knight in the world, is entitled to take his place there. As the legend evolved, this privilege fell first to Perceval, and later to Galahad.

The death of Arthur

When this period of chivalry was over, Arthur received from Rome a demand for the tribute which, it alleged, Britain owed the Empire since its conquest by Julius Caesar. Arthur contested the demand, referring to a number of glorious episodes during the course of which it was Britain, on the contrary, which had dominated the Empire. He then assembled his army, calling on the support of all his vassals and knights. Leaving behind Modred, the youngest of his nephews (and also his son by his half-sister), and Guinevere, who was to act as regent in his absence, he set sail for France. On his arrival he triumphed in single combat against the champion of Gaul, Frollo, then defeated the Romans and their eastern allies in a series of pitched battles. But just as he was preparing to cross Montjeu (the Alps) and march on Rome, he learnt that Modred had married Guinevere and usurped the throne.

Arthur returned speedily with his army and met the enemy, now allied to the Saxons, on the battlefield at Camlann, or, according to the later romance versions of the story, on Salisbury Plain. Only two of Arthur's knights survived the conflict. Arthur and Modred inflicted fatal wounds on one another, and Guinevere, who had fled on learning of Arthur's return (having

In the earliest texts it was at Camlann (possibly Camboglanna, a Roman fort on Hadrian's Wall) that Arthur lost his life fighting the Saxons (or pagans), as depicted in this 14th-century miniature (below). The 12th-century romances, however, substitute Salisbury for Camlann and introduce the figure of Modred into the story. This second battle of Salisbury has a symbolic significance, since it brings to a close the Arthurian golden age that began when Uther Pendragon conquered the Saxons at Salisbury and became king in place of his dead brother.

supposed him dead), died shortly after taking the veil. Since Arthur died without a direct heir, Cador, Duke of Cornwall, became the new king of Britain.

The cyclical romances of the 13th century, which drew on the Arthurian legend and fleshed it out in great detail, also modified the final episodes, including the 'Breton hope'. Suppressing references to the conflict with Rome, they place the emphasis instead on

Above: Modred and Arthur at the last battle. In order to fight Arthur, Modred (a Christian) joins ranks with the (pagan) Saxons, thus flouting the aspirations of his father and grandfather.

individual adventures, and a national perspective based on warfare and conquest is lacking in the majority of the prose texts. Moreover, they introduce major changes into the original scenario through their development of the figure of Lancelot. In this rewriting of the final catastrophe, Modred and Agravain expose the adultery of Lancelot and Guinevere, whom they catch in flagrante delicto. Eventually Arthur takes his wife back and goes to fight Lancelot in Brittany. At this juncture, Arthur learns that Modred, who has remained in Britain as regent, has usurped the throne and is seeking to marry the queen. Arthur returns to England and, despite being outnumbered by Modred's army, joins battle with his enemy on Salisbury Plain. In the ensuing slaughter

Death Barge of Arthur by Joseph Noel Paton (1862) shows Arthur's female attendants indulging in wild demonstrations of grief. The figures of the rowers are dressed as monks and bring a Christian note to the scene, but they are also reminiscent of Charon, the ferryman, who, in Greek legend, carries the souls of the dead to the underworld.

both armies are destroyed to the last man. Modred strikes Arthur a mortal blow and dies himself at Arthur's hand.

Meanwhile, Arthur leaves the battlefield, accompanied by the last two survivors. Overcome with despair, he suffocates one of them in a final embrace and orders the other to throw his sword into a nearby lake to prevent it falling into the wrong hands. At Bedivere's third attempt to carry out Arthur's wishes, a hand rises up out of the water, catches the sword and brandishes it towards heaven. Interpreting this as a portent of his impending death, Arthur dismisses Bedivere. Bedivere leaves him, but, overcome with curiosity, he looks back and sees a ship arriving across the sea with many beautiful women on board, and among them he recognizes Arthur's sister Morgan le Fay. The ship disappears into the west, carrying the body of Arthur. A few days later, the knight arrives at an abbey and is shown a new tomb. Arthur's body, he is told, was brought the evening before by a group of weeping women and now lies in the tomb. The 'Breton hope' is therefore an illusion: 'good King Arthur' is not living still on the isle of Avalon, and Arthur's tomb is there for all to visit in the grounds of a well-known abbey.

Below: Bedivere throwing the sword into the lake, from a 14th-century miniature. Since Arthur dies without an heir and no one else is competent to handle Excalibur, the sword must be returned to the Other World from where it came. The hand that rises out of the lake to catch the sword brandishes it three times in homage to the dying king.

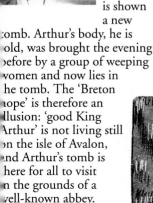

Is Arthur dead?

*L*eft: *The Sleep of King Arthur in Avalon* by Edward Burne-Jones (begun 1881). Compared with the seductive legend of the 'Breton hope', the notion of Arthur's tomb held little appeal for the 12th and 13th centuries. Several questions remained unanswered. Where was this tomb, and was it certain that the king's body was buried there? Who had deposited the body in the tomb – the ladies of Avalon or Bedivere and Girflet, the last Knights of the Round Table? And was Guinevere buried alongside her husband? In one of the romances Guinevere dies before Arthur, so that the king's body is taken to his wife's tomb.

*P*receding pages: *La Morte d'Arthur*, painting by James Archer (1861). The Pre-Raphaelites were sometimes casual about textual accuracy and the detail of the Grail in Archer's painting (top right) is anachronistic, since by the time Arthur dies it has already been taken up to heaven. It is also unclear whether at this point Arthur's female attendants have tried, and failed, to heal his wounds or whether the king is still alive as they prepare now to take him to Avalon.

The Arthurian legend brings together a number of different motifs from folklore, out of which it builds a relatively coherent structure. In the figure of Arthur we see a fusion of several traditions and cultural elements: Celtic mythology, the classical heritage, feudalism and the Christian tradition.

CHAPTER 4

FEUDALISM AND CHIVALRY

Opposite: the tournament, during which a knight demonstrated his prowess to the king and the ladies of the court watching from the upper balconies, was an essential part of the chivalrous life at Camelot, as was the ritual of knighting itself (right). During the Middle Ages Christian symbols were increasingly associated with knighting.

From Charlemagne's Peers to the Round Table

The literary model for Arthur and his Round Table is provided by Charlemagne and his twelve Peers. Arthur, as he appears in the *Historia regum Britanniae* and even in Wace's *Roman de Brut*, is a feudal sovereign, whose power is limited by the influence of his barons: he was known as the sovereign *primus inter pares* (first among equals). What this meant in practice was that the king was elected from among a number of high-ranking noblemen, who exercised almost equal authority to his own, and that he governed by their agreement and could take no decision that ran counter to their interests. The tension inherent in this hierarchical system is clear from the romances that describe the revolt of Britain's most illustrious noblemen against the young King Arthur, whose lineage is unknown to them. The Round Table, as it was originally conceived, precisely symbolizes this situation: there is in fact no place of honour at a round table, and all the knights are situated at the same level. Subsequently, however, the notion of the Round Table became more abstract. On a symbolic level it signified membership of a chivalrous elite characterized by its prowess and its courtliness. The Knights of the Round Table are not obliged, like the twelve Peers, to remain in their sovereign's entourage: on the contrary, they

The Round Table (opposite), in the Great Hall in Winchester Castle carries a portrait of Arthur and the names of twenty-four knights. For many years it was thought to be the Round Table of the 5th-century 'historical' Arthur, but when the table was restored in 1976 it was discovered to date from the second half of the 13th century (having no doubt been constructed under Henry III). The portrait of Arthur dates from the 16th century and was probably commissioned by Henry VIII. These discoveries demonstrate the continuing importance of the legend, and the efforts of English sovereigns to be associated with the story of Arthur.

regularly leave the court to embark on some new adventure. The spirit of community that characterizes the *chanson de geste* (Old French epic poems that celebrate heroism) and marks the high point of feudalism gives way to a more individual and individualistic conception of the function of chivalry.

Opposite: crowned emperor in AD 800 by the Pope himself, Charlemagne always retained the advantage over Arthur, whose march on Rome was halted by the news of Modred's treachery.

Arthur, symbol of feudalism

Arthur, the 'king who makes knights', as Chrétien
de Troyes' Perceval calls him, is the guarantor of this
system where individuals pursue their own goals while
remaining ready to respond to a summons from the king
in times of war. The court is the centre of the Arthurian
universe, and young men of an age to be knighted come
flocking to receive their arms from the hand of Arthur
himself. The original picture we have of Arthur is of
an outstanding warrior, who leads his armies to victory,
whether against the Saxons or the Romans, and who
personally enters the fray on numerous occasions.

Later, however, Arthur relinquishes his active role,
becoming instead a symbol of royal power, a static figure

The king would often
receive homage
from a new knight to
whom he had just given
his spurs. It was for this
reason that Lancelot,
already in love with
Guinevere and anxious
to avoid becoming
Arthur's vassal,
contrived to escape
the gift of the sword,
the most important
moment in the
ceremony.

Knighting was a solemn ritual involving a number of symbolic elements. The candidate, who had learnt to handle weapons as a squire in the service of an experienced knight, had to spend the night in prayer. The next day his lord handed him the sword with which it was his duty to defend the interests of the Church and those of the weak and disadvantaged (in particular ladies and young girls), along with his spurs. The sovereign

then dubbed him and embraced him. Following the ceremony new knights would demonstrate their prowess by taking part in a light-hearted joust known as a quintain.

Above: sculpture of Arthur's head.

who presides over the feasts and tournaments at Camelot, his legendary castle. His life is too precious to risk in the way that the ordinary knight will risk his by embarking on dangerous adventures; besides, Arthur has a clearly determined function, which is to reign, while the more active figures of the court gravitate around him. As a number of 13th-century texts suggest, if the king fails in his duties, that is, primarily his obligation to bestow largesse on his knights, the latter leave his court, and the court falls into decline.

The influence of the feudal pattern can even be felt in the assimilation of pre-existing material drawn from the romances relating to Tristan. The story of Tristan presents some difficulties for the new model: since Arthur is king of the whole of Britain, which obviously includes Cornwall; but King Mark, Tristan's uncle, and husband of Queen Isolde, is always designated as King of Cornwall. As a means of reconciling these apparently incompatible versions, Mark is represented as a minor king, a high-ranking nobleman who answers to Arthur, the only true king in Britain and the border territories.

Courtliness and 'fin'amor'

Unlike Charlemagne, Arthur is more than simply a warrior king: he is the symbol and perfect expression of a world of chivalry that is also a world governed by the principles of courtly behaviour, that new ideology imported from the South of France by the troubadours who accompanied Eleanor of Aquitaine on the occasion of two successive marriages. The basic rules of courtly behaviour differ little from Christian precepts: a knight must place himself in the service of the widow and the orphan; he must behave honourably at all times, respecting the rights of the individual and, where necessary, ensuring that these rights are respected by others. But the principal emphasis of courtly behaviour relates to the conduct to be observed vis-à-vis ladies and young women. If Gawain's inveterate tendency to flirt with every young woman he meets constitutes a reprehensible attitude in the eyes of the Church, the

Below: Tristan and Isolde accidentally drink this magic potion, prepared by Isolde's mother, while crossing the sea to meet King Mark of Cornwall, Tristan's uncle, to whom Isolde is betrothed.

principles of *fin'amor* – 'serious' courtly love – are downright scandalous, since this perfect love is necessarily adulterous, and the lover is nevertheless obliged to submit entirely to the whims of his lady.

The love triangle

From the outset King Arthur is presented as married, in accordance with the traditional image of the good sovereign. Queen Guinevere is probably an adaptation of the mythical figure of Sovereignty – a fact that

Above: Guinevere and Lancelot embracing. *Fin'amor* placed the woman in a superior position with regard to her lover, who received her love (usually symbolic rather than concrete) only in exchange for total devotion.

'The most beautiful lady in the world'

Medieval descriptions of feminine beauty are based on a handful of commonplaces: golden hair, shining eyes, snow-white skin, crimson lips, and teeth like pearls. Guinevere (left) and Isolde (opposite) occupy the same position in the structural framework of their respective romances, and the similarities in their descriptions are particularly striking. One of the favourite pastimes of the 'late' prose romances of the 13th century was to establish a hierarchy of feminine beauty and chivalry. Their authors speak, for example, of the second and third most beautiful woman in the world, and the eighth best knight. In the prose *Tristan*, Lancelot and Tristan vie with one another in modesty, willingly conceding to the other the title of 'best knight', but each is ready to take up arms against the other to defend his respective lady's claim to the title 'the most beautiful lady'. Left: *Queen Guinevere*, a painting by William Morris. Opposite: *Queen Guinevere's Maying*, a painting by John Collier.

'Good lady' or 'false serpent'

Merlin was particularly ill-fated in his choice of pupils. After agreeing to teach his magic arts to Morgan le Fay (opposite page, painted by Frederick Sandys) in exchange for her love, he fell in love with a young 'huntress', probably an incarnation of the goddess Diana, and entered into the same agreement with her. But Nimue, or Viviane, as Tennyson calls her (seen here, left, with Merlin in a painting by Edward Burne-Jones), takes a violent dislike to this 'son of the devil' who simply wants to rob her of her virginity. She succeeds in walling him into a tomb – or 'prison of air', in the more courtly version – so that he can never leave her and seduce other young women, but is then overcome with remorse and endeavours to continue the work of the enchanted magician by protecting Arthur and his knights. As the Lady of the Lake, she abducts the young Lancelot and gives him a courtly education in her castle disguised as a lake.

explains her tendency to be abducted by every pretender to the throne. In the *Historia* and the *Brut*, although she fails to produce an heir, she is shown to be a good wife (in other words, a faithful one), until she betrays the king by becoming the wife of the usurper Modred – and even then it remains unclear from the texts whether this betrayal is voluntary or whether the queen is simply taken hostage by the traitor.

In the romances, however, Guinevere undergoes a change of image. In *Le Chevalier de la charrette*, the prose romance written by Chrétien de Troyes, the 12th-century French poet from Champagne, Lancelot (Chrétien's invention) appears as the queen's lover – as well, of course, as best knight in the world. It is because of this adulterous love that Lancelot is unable to succeed in the quest for the Grail, and ultimately that the Arthurian dream comes to an end. The code of chivalry relied, however, on the defence of Christian virtues and, despite his anger towards Guinevere, Arthur is obliged to take her back when the Church demands it on pain of excommunication.

Christian tradition and Celtic legend meet

Arthur, like Charlemagne (if to a lesser degree), is a Christian king with a duty to defend the Christian faith;

Above left: Lancelot kissing Guinevere for the first time, in an early 15th-century French miniature. The figure on the left is Galehaut, Prince of the Far-Away Isles. Having renounced the idea of conquering Arthur's kingdom in order to win Lancelot's friendship, he discovers the secret of his love for the queen and succeeds in uniting the two lovers in the most generous manner.

Morgan, who is the sworn enemy of her half-brother and Queen Guinevere (although the reasons for this hostility are never given in the romances), holds Lancelot prisoner in her castle. To pass the time during his long months of captivity, Lancelot paints scenes from his adulterous relationship with Queen Guinevere on the walls of his prison. Later, during a visit by King Arthur, Morgan takes pleasure in showing him the frescoes (left).

he is the secular arm of the Church and the instrument of God. And although there is no 'crusade', properly speaking, in the Arthurian legend, Arthur is fighting a pagan enemy.

But the body of Arthurian literature also belongs to an older, Celtic and pagan tradition linking Arthur with the pantheon of Celtic gods and interpreting the stories dedicated to him in a mythical light. The presence of an early King Arthur is mentioned in certain Irish and Welsh texts, which provide evidence of a legend that predates the material preserved in the literary texts. Arthur's sword, according to this tradition, is called Caledwlch, from which the famous Excalibur is clearly derived.

The clearest link between Arthur and the Celtic myths is undoubtedly provided by his sister, known according to the legend as 'Morgan le Fay'. Morgan, the fairy-lover, was in the original probably an incarnation of the Great Mother Goddess, whose incestuous union with the king ensures the fertility of the earth. This explains the conflict between Morgan and Guinevere, another image of the goddess as an incarnation of sovereignty, the feminine principle with which the king must unite physically in order to acquire the right to exercise power.

In the prose romances Lancelot's relationship with Guinevere spans almost thirty years, whereas in Chrétien de Troyes it is limited to a single night of ecstasy. The later works therefore include a number of episodes that are mere padding. Lancelot spends his life either looking for adventures or in captivity, only meeting the queen infrequently. They communicate through intermediaries, and send one another objects symbolizing their love, such as the ring that Guinevere entrusts to Bohort in this (centre) mid-15th-century French miniature.

Since the 19th century Merlin (far left) has generally been represented as a respectable old man dressed in the long, flowing robes of a magician. But in the medieval texts he is above all the 'wise child', making his first prophecies from the age of seven, and also the illusionist, capable of assuming whatever form he pleases (including that of a stag) and never revealing his true face. King Arthur (centre) is rarely represented in armour in medieval illuminated manuscripts: more often than not he appears wearing a crown and sitting on his throne, presiding over some major event such as a banquet or a tournament. In her youth Morgan (left) was supposedly the most beautiful young woman in the world, but when she learnt the necromancer's arts from Merlin – so entering a pact with the devil – she grew hideous and used spells to blind her many 'friends' to her ugliness. Left: embroidered figures by William Morris, based on drawings by Edward Burne-Jones.

The Grail

The clearest sign of Arthur's progressive transformation into the defender of the Christian faith is in the link established between the king and the Grail, which Chrétien de Troyes was the first to associate with the Arthurian legend. Unfortunately, we cannot be sure even now what was meant by the word 'Grail', much less what '*the* Grail' signified. Originally a magic vessel used for serving food or administering medicines, the Grail later acquired powerful Christian connotations, becoming (with Robert de Boron) the chalice in which Joseph of Arimathea collected the blood of Christ on the Cross. As leader of the Knights of the Round Table who embark on the quest for the 'Holy' Grail, Arthur clearly demonstrates his status

Above: Joseph of Arimathea collecting Christ's blood Christ had used the same cup to consecrate the wine at the Last Supper. In the Middle Ages Joseph was regarded (logically enough) as the first priest. During his long years in captivity at the hands of the Jews, he received visions of the Grail (left) and was kept alive through the grace it bestowed upon him. He reappears in the *Queste del Saint Graal* as one of the mystical figures who perform the sacred rites in the service of the Grail at Corbenic

s a Christian king. And yet the distinction between 'spiritual' chivalry, which admits the aspirant into the mysteries of the Grail, and 'earthly' chivalry, based on chivalric and courtly attitudes deriving from an earlier tradition, demonstrates just how superficial this Christianization really is.

Rex quondam rexque futurus: 'the once and future king'

Nevertheless, through his association with two separate systems of representation, two symbolic worlds, Arthur becomes a memorable figure who exerts a powerful influence on the cultural imagination: he is the *rex quondam rexque futurus*, the 'king of former days' who is also 'the king to come' (or, in the title of T. H. White's classic tale, 'the once and future king'). While acquiring Christlike associations, he also retains characteristics of what was probably his earliest incarnation as a Celtic divinity.

The Christian connections become more pronounced over time, so that by the end of the Middle Ages Arthur finds a place in the widely represented series of the 'Nine Worthies', appearing alongside Charlemagne and Godefroy de Bouillon, the conqueror of Jerusalem during the First Crusade, as an embodiment of one of the three best Christian knights. These three Christian heroes, regarded as historical personages, rub shoulders with three heroes from Antiquity (Hector of Troy, Alexander the Great and Julius Caesar) and three biblical heroes (King David, Joshua and Judas Maccabaeus).

It is also worth noting that Godefroy de Bouillon became the subject of a romance associated in particular with the legend of the Knight and the Swan.

The Grail is not integral to the Arthurian legend and is not mentioned in either the *Historia regum Britanniae* or Wace's *Roman de Brut*. The two great themes of Breton literature were fused under the influence of the Cistercians in the 13th century and 'classical' chivalry came to be regarded as an imperfect stage in Christian chivalry, as embodied in the *militia Dei* dear to Bernard of Clairvaux (in reality the military monastic orders like the Templars and the Hospitallers). Below: Charlemagne and Arthur in the 'Nine Worthies' series.

B dist li contes que quant li
relos fu entres en la forest per
louse quit cheuaucha tant q̃
sotaus fu leues t lors en ọtri

It was with Wace's *Roman de Brut* that the figure of Arthur first entered the realms of literature and began to exert its magnetic attraction. For almost a century and a half Arthurian 'romances' were to prove one of the richest genres of the French Middle Ages, and every country in Europe borrowed from the legend, either drawing on it, or reproducing the stories wholesale, translating or adapting them to regional tastes.

CHAPTER 5

AN EXTRAORDINARY LITERARY FLOWERING

Left: Arthur's knights often test their skill and courage by fighting lions, and Lancelot, 'the best knight in the world', is repeatedly engaged in this activity, which clearly has biblical and symbolic connotations. Right: Illuminated letter in the French *Lancelot* (1470).

Chrétien de Troyes

France was the first to adopt the Arthurian legend from the British Isles and develop it as a literary theme. King Arthur appears in some of Marie de France's lays (in a rather unflattering light), but it was only in the romances of Chrétien de Troyes that he became a central figure. This poet from Champagne was active roughly between the years 1165 and 1190, first at the court of Countess Marie de Champagne, daughter of Eleanor of Aquitaine, then later, if

we are to believe the prologue to the *Conte du Graal*, in the service of Count Philip of Flanders. Of Chrétien's five romances, four (*Erec et Enide*, *Le Chevalier de la charrette*, *Le Chevalier au lion* and *Le Conte du Graal*) are resolutely Arthurian: they deal with the 'matter of Britain', recounting the adventures of Arthur's knights, who gravitate back to his court after confronting various ordeals from which they emerge triumphant. They deal with the legend's key figures: the king himself, his nephew Gawain, the seneschal Kay and Queen Guinevere.

The medieval illuminator generally set to work once the copyist had finished (as proved by those incomplete manuscripts where the spaces reserved for the miniatures have been left blank) and, by merely referring to the rubrics or chapter

headings, occasionally produced something inappropriate. The 13th and 14th centuries introduced greater sophistication, with a series of vignettes illustrating the different stages of a narrative sequence. Opposite top and above: miniatures from *Le Chevalier au Lion* (or *Yvain*) by Chrétien de Troyes. Main picture: Perceval arriving at the castle of the Holy Grail, miniature from *Le Conte du Graal* by Chrétien de Troyes.

The last of these romances, *Le Conte du Graal*, is unfinished and has spawned a number of other texts that continue the story. It introduces a new theme in the shape of the Grail, which it relates to the Arthurian world through the intermediary of an unknown knight, Perceval the Welshman.

Christianization

At the end of the 12th century an event occurred that was to have far-reaching consequences for literary history. A certain Robert de Boron (whose name was artificially constructed out of other names that appear in the Grail texts and who almost certainly never existed) composed a sort of verse prologue to the *Conte du Graal* which gives the text a resolutely Christian interpretation.

This was followed by a trilogy entitled the *Joseph d'Arimathie* (edited under the title *Le Roman de l'Estoire du Graal*), the *Merlin* and the *Perceval*, which made a link between the time of Christ and the Arthurian epic. The second part relates the story of the Grail and of Joseph of Arimathea to that of Arthur and the Round Table by making a few adjustments along the way. It interprets the Round Table in essentially religious terms, describing it as a reproduction of the table used at the Last Supper and of the Grail table which Joseph of Arimathea devised on Christ's instructions as a means of distinguishing the elect from their weaker companions during the Grail's long journey to the West.

The original link between Arthur and the Grail is rather tenuous: Perceval, the Chosen One, is simply a knight from Arthur's entourage, though he remains largely a stranger to the court while pursuing a highly individual quest for the Grail castle, to which he attaches an obscure and complicated family history. When he reaches the end of his quest, it is likely that in

Above: Perceval's encounter with a group of knights.

he early versions Perceval becomes the new king of the Grail, within a framework that is only loosely Arthurian.

From the moment that the Grail and the Round Table are given Christian associations, Arthur's court becomes a Christian court and his knights invariably become Christian heroes – though their new Christian status sits uneasily with their Celtic origins, since the Celts' value system differed widely from the Christian one. Only a small handful of chosen ones can make this change successfully, and one of the major causes for the final disaster that destroys the kingdom of Logres and all that Arthur has worked for is this excessive Christianization of the old Celtic models and the introduction of the Grail into the adventures of the Round Table.

Above: Chrétien de Troyes introduces a number of strange elements into the Grail procession: young men carrying candlesticks and a 'bleeding' lance, a young woman bearing the Grail, and another with a small silver tray (which is replaced by a broken sword). The 13th-century versions feature Joseph of Arimathea and angels in place of the acolytes.

The holy quest

The introduction of the Grail legend turns the courtly hierarchy upside down, so that the 'courtliest' knights, like Gawain, become the libertines who fail to reach the castle where the Grail is housed (left). Perceval is similarly compromised by his dealings with *fin'amor* and is supplanted by the chaste Galahad, who succeeds in the quest and in so doing eliminates all the supernatural trials, the 'wonders'. Arthur seems well aware of the danger that the Grail poses for him and his court, since the texts record his despair when all his knights swear to take up the quest for a year and a day (preceding pages). In the prose texts the castle of Corbenic attracts as many visitors as any other location in the Arthurian world, but the sacred object only appears to those who have shown themselves worthy. Gawain, for example, though a paragon of traditional courtly virtues, fails because, instead of praying, he becomes distracted by the beauty of the Grail bearer. Previous page, this page and overleaf: tapestries after designs by Edward Burne-Jones.

The different manifestations of the Grail

The Grail has several aspects, that is to say that its contents vary for all those fortunate enough to see it; and even within an individual vision the object metamorphoses itself according to a curiously dreamlike logic. Some claim that it contains a chalice (although it is in itself a chalice) or a candle, which was a rarity at the time. Galahad, the most important of the trinity of 'holy knights' – a grouping that replicates the Holy Trinity and includes Perceval and Lancelot's devout cousin Bohort – is the only one of the three to glimpse the secrets of the Grail (below left). But the mystery cannot be expressed – 'No tongue could tell, and no pen write, the holy secrets of the Grail' – and the reader's curiosity is never satisfied. Left above: the Round Table.

ors regardent entraus qui
dir il sont · Et anccuent kil
sont · xxv· par contre · caetui
monte soi son æual · Et puis prendet

si mal amene kil na mestier de mi
car il est naurez amort · Et li aut
ki apres tenotent · se fierent ent
les autres · Et en abatent pite · Et

From verse to prose

Arthurian literature developed in a cumulative way. Each new text supplemented earlier ones to compose a vast fresco 'realistically' reproducing a complete and coherent universe in all its richness and variety. The verse romances only partially resolved the mystery surrounding the Grail, but they were nevertheless followed in the 13th century by a series of romances based on heroic adventures (often with Gawain as the hero), all of which belong to the Arthurian genre.

However, between the *Estoire del Saint Graal* and the *Merlin* a significant shift occurred when the octosyllable in rhyming couplets (alternate masculine and feminine) yielded to prose. Verse had come to be regarded as too literary – in other words, too closely allied to invention – and it was thought that no one writing in verse could possibly be telling the truth. The prose romance, on the other hand, imitated the Latin prose of the chronicles and was thereby guaranteed an intrinsic veracity – and given the fact that the new narrative material was fairly hard to believe, anything that vouchsafed for its truthfulness was a valuable asset. Prose was also a closer approximation to the style of the New Testament, and in particular the Gospels, and – though it was never openly admitted – the ambition of the Grail romances, composed as they were under the influence of the Cistercians, was to create a new Gospel, as worthy of belonging to the canon as its predecessors. It was not merely the texts dedicated to the Grail legend

As the embodiment of Sovereignty, Guinevere was frequently abducted by pretenders to the throne; here she is being rescued by Lancelot.

at mimicked the style of the chronicles: all the
rthurian literature (it became in fact virtually
mpossible to differentiate between the two) was written
n prose from now on and claimed strictly to reproduce
hronicles composed in the time of Arthur himself,
hose accuracy, therefore, was beyond question. It was
hrough prose alone, conceived as a mode of analytical
ther than imaginative expression, that the rich
bundance of reality could be recaptured, in accurate
nd thorough detail, free of any superfluous
mbellishment.

ompilations and compendia

uring the 13th century an attempt was made to
rovide an exhaustive account of the multiplicity of the

On Whit Sunday, while all the Knights of the Round Table are assembled in honour of the new knight Galahad, who has installed himself in the Perilous Seat, they have a mystical vision of the Grail (below) and a succession of delicious dishes appears before the assembled company. This was the first and only mention of the Grail's appearance other than at Corbenic at this date, although later texts tend to present the Grail (with unwitting humour) as 'itinerant' – provider of a kind of supernatural catering service.

world in every field of learning, a massive undertaking that led to the production of numerous *miroirs* (mirrors), encyclopaedias gathering together in a single volume all the knowledge that had been acquired on a certain subject. The romance was caught up in the same development, so that relatively short narratives describing the more noteworthy adventures of an isolated individual gave way to massive works written from multiple points of view, interweaving separate narrative threads and recounting adventures spanning several decades and involving dozens of different heroes. The romances, which had averaged some six or seven thousand lines of verse, now ran to hundreds of pages of prose. And, to compound matters, they were organized into cycles covering an entire period or life. The end of the century saw the production of massive compilations, of varying interest, in which the reader is not spared a single episode, however slight, but learns in the minutest detail how figures of secondary importance employ their time in the course of their various adventures.

The *Lancelot-Graal* cycle

Written in the 13th century by an anonymous author, the *Lancelot-Graal* cycle is the first of the prose cycles after the *Estoire del Saint Graal* and the *Merlin*. In the central section, the two-thousand-page *Lancelot*, the action is situated early in Arthur's reign and principally revolves around the adventures of Lancelot of the Lake. The transition from the *Lancelot* to the *Queste del Saint Graal* – which gives the legend its Christian focus – is carried out without any attempt at continuity.

Deceived by the Fisher King's daughter in the guise of Guinevere, Lancelot begets the future hero of the Grail quest, Galahad the Pure, who is brought up by his mother and grandfather. On the eve of Whit Sunday Galahad asks his father to knight him. Lancelot carries out his wish (above), torn between pride in his son and sorrow at losing his claim to knightly pre-eminence.

Accompanied by Perceval and Lancelot's cousin Bohort, Lancelot's son Galahad is granted a glimpse of the mysteries of the Holy Grail. Galahad and Perceval die, since to know such ecstacy and to continue to live an earthly existence is impossible. Bohort returns to Arthur's court to report on what has happened, and the last part of the cycle, *La Mort le roi Artu*, brings the legend to a drastic close by killing off all the characters who have survived the quest for the Grail: after the religious apotheosis comes the secular tragedy, which describes the end of the Arthurian world with painful intensity.

This literary monument was composed from 1225 to 1230. Given its size, it seems unlikely that it was the work of a single person, although we

Below left: Galahad and Perceval arriving at the castle of Carceloi. Below: Galahad, Perceval and Bohort on their way to Sarras in their magical boat. Below bottom: Bohort telling Arthur about the death of Galahad and Perceval.

have no evidence to suggest that it was written by a number of people. It was soon imitated by a second cycle, the Post-Vulgate cycle (only fragments of which remain), which tells the same story but in a different style.

Meanwhile, the enduring popularity of the Tristan legend led to the composition of an enormous prose romance linking the Cornish lovers with the Arthurian world – even going so far as to make Tristan a Knight of the Round Table.

genr ⁊ touche ale

a oou fait li se cent

a legne de ses matte

plainc ⁊ mierueil

Si com lanſ' uit le ſaut graal ⁊ li
auint puis en mains lius · ⁊ li

A bians sire der loœs loueſ
nous garis lui · ⁊ ne demou
va gairet que il sen dort. ꝯ gnt

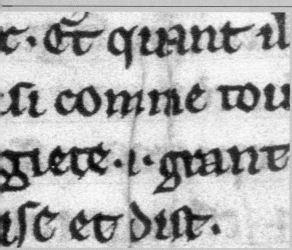

Prose authentification

The Arthurian legend had been so 'corrupted' by poets more concerned with aesthetic invention than with truth that no one any longer believed a word of it. What was needed was a guarantee of authenticity through the medium of prose. Indeed, Wace felt that storytellers had told so many stories that everything sounded like a lie. Prose was rhetorical; it rejected the false attractions of the written word and aimed to achieve transparency. Since all literary activity was regarded as suspect, it became indispensable to appeal to an apparently neutral form of communication, one that was tacitly authorized by a vision of the world thoroughly steeped in Christian orthodoxy. Prose that imitated Latin was thus thought to give a seal of authenticity to the most outlandish adventures, since it placed the text in line with the historical chronicles and above all the Bible, or more precisely the Gospels. Left: Lancelot praying in a miniature taken from one of the manuscripts that make up the huge prose cycle of the *Lancelot-Graal*.

Tristan

The romance of 'Tristan and Isolde'

After triumphing over the giant-sized warrior Morholt of Ireland, Tristan wins the hand of the Irish princess Isolde for his uncle, King Mark. Tristan and Isolde inadvertently drink a magic potion and fall in love. The jealous barons inform King Mark and the two lovers are condemned to death. They escape to the forest, but are later reconciled with the king. Tristan goes to live in Brittany, where he marries the duke's daughter, Isolde of the White Hands, 'on account of her beauty and her name', but, tormented with love for the other Isolde, he never consummates the marriage. Dying from a wound, he sends his friend Kaherdin to fetch the queen from Cornwall, but Isolde of the White Hands tells him that the ship arriving from Cornwall is carrying black sails (a sign that Isolde has not come); Tristan dies of grief and Isolde, arriving too late, dies at his side. Opposite above: Tristan and Isolde on the ship taking them to Cornwall. Opposite below: 13th-century ivory casket representing the two lovers. Main picture: Tristan fighting Palamedes.

In terms of their spatio-temporal framework the *Lancelot-Graal* and the prose *Tristan* are identical and the latter work provides a successful example of the way in which the legend was developed.

The late texts

Since all the legendary characters are dead by the end of the *Mort Artu*, and most of them have died without leaving an heir, there was no question of a sequel. The only option was to look to the past, and several new romances are situated in the time of Uther Pendragon. One of the last great Arthurian prose romances of the Middle Ages (composed during the first half of the 14th century), *Perceforest*

describes the reign of the two kings Betis Perceforest and Gadiffer of Scotland, companions of Alexander the Great who have been miraculously swept on to Britain's shores at a time when the island is in need of a new ruler. This interesting version thus has Alexander spend a period of his life in Britain and makes him the ancestor of Arthur.

Closer to the Arthurian golden age, the great *Palamedes* revolves around the heroic exploits of King Meliadus of Loenois, the father of Tristan. These 'Breton' rather than Arthurian romances do not, by definition, introduce the figures of King Arthur and his regular entourage; but the frame of reference is Arthurian, and it was to remain so until the very end of the Middle Ages.

The story of Meliadus has as its principal hero Tristan's father, the King of Loenois (a kingdom on the border with Cornwall), who falls in love with King Mark's sister and abducts her when she falls pregnant. In these late texts Mark is depicted as a negative character overcome with hatred for worthy knights, and as cowardly as he is vindictive. True to character, therefore, he sets out to kill his sister's lover during a tournament – generally a light-hearted affair intended as entertainment only (above, Meliadus and Tristan fighting). Mark subsequently kills the husband of another sister and seeks to dispose of her son, whose literary appearance is cut short as a result.

From Layamon's *Brut* to the romance *Of Arthour and of Merlin*

The most spectacular development of Arthurian themes occurred in Britain – not surprisingly, perhaps, since the 'historical' Arthur was associated with Britain and King Arthur made his first literary appearance in an Anglo-Norman work. While this early literature of Britain was written in Anglo-Norman, the narrative material linked to the legend of Arthur soon found linguistic roots on the site of the most famous episodes of the Arthurian adventure.

A work based on Wace's *Brut* – part translation, part adaptation (and bearing the same title) – appeared in English at the very beginning of the 13th century, signed by a certain Layamon.

In the course of the century this was followed by a number of verse texts which borrowed their plots from the French texts – either directly, like the romance *Of Arthour and of Merlin*, which basically recounts the circumstances of Arthur's birth and accession to the throne, while mixing traditional elements with original themes; or in a looser fashion by simply using the framework of the legend and its principal characters, the best example being the celebrated *Sir Gawain and the Green Knight*.

Celtic literature, and in particular Welsh literature, was

In *Sir Gawain and the Green Knight* the Green Knight, a semi-supernatural being, proposes to Gawain that he cut off the Knight's head, saying that in a year's time he will return and cut off his. Gawain inevitably emerges triumphant from the 'beheading game', which has been arranged (though we never learn why) by Morgan Le Fay.

simultaneously drawing on the same material, which, some said, rightfully belonged to it.

The problem of the antecedence of the Welsh texts in relation to the Continental romances is virtually impossible to resolve, since, even if the manuscripts of the *Mabinogion* – those Welsh tales with a strongly Arthurian flavour – are clearly more recent than the works of Chrétien de Troyes, it can always be argued that earlier versions existed and that Continental writers drew their inspiration from them via the intermediary of the Breton storytellers.

Below: introduction from a 1529 edition of Malory's *Morte d'Arthur*. The *Morte d'Arthur* succeeded in fusing the French *Lancelot-Graal* cycle with later romances like the prose *Tristan*, depicting Tristan as a fully fledged Knight of the Round Table and devoting an entire book

Malory and Caxton

It was not until the 15th century, however, that the Arthurian legend really came into its own in England. Sir Thomas Malory's *Morte d'Arthur*, a work of impressively panoramic proportions, whose 'French' title helped to guarantee its success, was inspired by the 14th-century alliterative *Morte Arthure*, and by French sources (the *Lancelot-Graal*) and later compilations, and was said to have been composed as a means of whiling

to him. Malory generally reproduces important episodes from earlier works in their entirety, even if he radically reorganizes the material and, in particular, adjusts the chronology of events.

...way the gloomy hours of Malory's imprisonment for political reasons. The work was finished in 1470, but not published until it was printed by Caxton in 1485. For many years critical commentaries were based exclusively on the Caxton version, which provided the basis for subsequent editions, and it was not until recently that the discrepancies between Malory's text and Caxton's have come to light. Malory's work was the first to bring together the different strands of the Arthurian legend into one connected narrative. Printed editions in French from the great cycles, of which there were a number after 1492, were limited to single volumes.

By using the sequence of Lancelot mounting the cart (bottom right) Malory reproduces the central scene in Chrétien de Troyes' *Le Chevalier de la charrette*, where we are first introduced to Lancelot of the Lake. Left: detail illustrating Lancelot's madness. Centre: Merlin under Nimue's spell. Bottom left: the birth of Tristan.

King A[

OR,

The Britiſh Worthy.

A *Dramatick*

OPERA.

Perform'd at the *QUEENS* Theatre

Spenser and Purcell

Malory's great work restored to Britain a part of its national heritage, which was henceforth to be jealously guarded. The legend of Arthur had found its way into the realms of literature and art. Shakespeare may not have drawn inspiration from the stories of the Round Table, but the figure of the *rex quondam rexque futurus* appears, for example, in *The Faerie Queene* by Edmund Spenser (1596), even if the original story is now unrecognizable. In Spenser's work it is not Arthur, but his twin brother, who plays a symbolic role and whose

Although Purcell's opera *King Arthur* (above, title page) has only the most tenuous of links with medieval Arthurian literature, it does show that the legend was still alive in England at the end of the 17th century (although it had disappeared in France by then).

THUR:

ontacts with the world of the fairies promote an nlightened reign, for the good of humanity, more or ess free from the trials that afflict the world of mortals. An equally fanciful evolution of the legend is to be found in the opera *King Arthur* by Henry Purcell (1691), which ignores the original details, simply retaining a few of the key figures such as Arthur and Merlin.

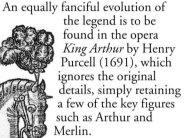

Spain, Portugal and Italy

The influence of the French romances was felt less in Italy, Spain and Portugal, where there was little reason for the figure of Arthur to appeal to the popular imagination. The Grail, however, was a subject of some curiosity in Spain (according to certain egends the sacred object was housed in a Pyrenean nonastery) and *La Queste del Saint Graal* was translated nto both Spanish and Portuguese under the title *Demanda del Sancto Grial*. Stories of knightly adventures ontinued to thrive longer in Spain than in France. t the end of the Middle Ages innumerable romances

Spenser develops his story in ways that have no connection with the framework of the Arthurian legend. What is quite evident in this monumental work that defies classification, and which is barely legible today, is the nostalgia for a past age when courtly virtues and chivalry were more important than commercial and political considerations. In this sense *The Faerie Queene* presents a utopia in which the figure of Arthur is simply the pretext for a composition outlining an improbable golden age. Left: the Knight with the Red Cross, an illustration from *The Faerie Queene*.

appeared describing the activities of knights close to the Arthurian model, even if the framework of the stories was not, and the *Amadis de Gaule* stories, translated in the 16th century, were enormously popular with a generation of French readers still able to appreciate the works of the 'Gothic' age. The interest in Arthurian romances was as superficial in Italy as it was in Spain and Portugal, but adaptations of existing sources did appear, including *La Tavola ritonda*.

Germany: towards the Grail

The situation was quite different in Germany, whose literature was closely affiliated with that of France, and the romances of Chrétien de Troyes were 'translated' into Middle High German shortly after their appearance in France, Chrétien's *Erec et Enide* and *Le Chevalier au lion* finding their counterparts in Hartmann von Aue's *Erec* and *Iwein*.

The decisive event, however, was the adaptation, in around 1200, of *Le Conte du Graal* by the epic poet Wolfram von Eschenbach. Unlike Hartmann's works, which remained relatively close to their model, the *Parzival* is an original work that develops the Grail

Interest in the Arthurian romances in Italy, and particularly the area around Venice, led to the production of numerous manuscripts of the *Lancelot-Graal* and the prose *Tristan*, copied in workshops (sometimes with the effect of Italianizing the language) and richly illustrated in the Italian style, as in this 14th-century miniature (left) showing Arthur arriving at Camelot.

Opposite: miniatures from *Parzival* showing the hero killing the Scarlet Knight and appropriating his arms; wounding Kay to avenge the young girl who had smiled at him; and contemplating three drops of blood in the snow which remind him of the face of his mistress Blanchefleur. The first part of Eschenbach's work, which describes the education of Perceval-Parzival, follows Chrétien de Troyes' *Conte du Graal* fairly closely. The German writer then demonstrates his originality by constructing around the Grail a political utopia founded on the knights and depicting the Grail itself as a mysterious stone endowed with very strange properties.

Overleaf: miniature from *Parzival*.

theme in surprising ways and uses it as the basis for a political utopia.

Parzival was followed by a number of other Arthurian romances of lesser importance: from Ulrich von Zatzikhoven's *Lanzelet* and Heinrich von dem Türlin's *Diû Crône*, which both introduce (with varying success) what appear to be Celtic motifs and episodes into the framework of the classic Arthurian narrative, to the nostalgic texts by Ulrich Fuetrer in the 15th century. There was also a *Prosa Lancelot*, which reproduces the central section of the *Lancelot-Graal*, but in a rather schematic form. The enthusiasm of the German public for the legend of King Arthur continued unabated until the 15th century.

At the beginning of the Renaissance, however, Arthur's star began to wane across Europe, even if it burned for a little longer in Britain than elsewhere. It was not until the 19th century and the advent of Romanticism, accompanied by a taste for the 'Gothic', that the stories of King Arthur and the Knights of the Round Table came into their own once more, giving rise to a movement which, though limited in France and Germany, was to enjoy tremendous popularity in Britain and the United States.

DOCUMENTS

Arthur in 12th-century literature

Before the events of his life were dramatized in the great prose romances of the 12th century, Arthur already existed in literature as a shadowy, symbolic figure – one who did not always appear to the best advantage.

Above: a stag hunt. Previous page: Merlin.

Arthur of Britain

In 1138 Geoffrey of Monmouth wrote the first significant literary text introducing the Arthurian figure to European literature, in which a favourable impression is given of the king.

Dubricius therefore, sorrowing over the calamities of the country, assembled the other prelates, and did invest Arthur with the crown of the realm. At that time Arthur was a youth of fifteen years of a courage and generosity beyond compare, whereunto his inborn goodness did lend such grace as that he was beloved of well-nigh all the peoples in the land. After he had been invested with the ensigns of royalty, he abided by his ancient wont, and was so prodigal of his bounties as that he began to run short of wherewithal to distribute amongst the huge multitude of knights that made repair unto him. But he that hath within him a bountiful nature along with prowess, albeit that he be lacking for a time, natheless in no wise shall poverty be his bane for ever. Wherefore did Arthur, for that in him did valour keep company with largesse, make resolve to harry the Saxons, to the end that with their treasure he might make rich the retainers that were of his own household. And herein was he monished of his own lawful right, seeing that of right ought he to hold the sovereignty of the whole island in virtue of his claim hereditary. Assembling, therefore, all the youth that were of his allegiance, he made first for York....

And when much of the day had been spent on this wise, Arthur waxed wroth at the stubbornness of their resistance, and the slowness of his own advance, and drawing forth Caliburn, his sword, crieth aloud the name of Holy Mary,

nd thrusteth him forward with a swift
nset into the thickest press of the
nemy's ranks. Whomsoever he
ouched, calling upon God, he slew at
single blow, nor did he once slacken
n his onslaught until that he had slain
our hundred and seventy men single-
anded with his sword Caliburn. This
vhen the Britons beheld, they followed
im up in close rank dealing slaughter
n every side....

And whilst that he was serving them
ut on this wise arrived Guillamur,
King of Ireland, with a mighty host
f barbarians in a fleet, to bring
uccour unto the wretched islanders.
Whereupon Arthur left off the leaguer
nd began to turn his arms against the
rish, whom he forced to return unto
heir own country, cut to pieces without
nercy. When he had won the victory,
e again gave all his thoughts to doing
way utterly the race of the Scots and
Picts, and yielded him to treating with
vith a cruelty beyond compare. Not
single one that he could lay hands on
lid he spare, insomuch as that at last
ll the bishops of the miserable country
ssembled together with all the clergy
f their obedience, and came unto him
arefoot, bearing relics of the saints and
he sacraments of the church, imploring
he King's mercy for the safety of their
eople. As soon as they came into his
resence, they prayed him on their
ended knees to have pity on the
own-trodden folk, for that he had
isited them with pains and penalties
now, nor was any need to cut off the
canty few that still survived to the
ast man. Some petty portion of the
ountry he might allot unto them
vhereon they might be allowed to
ear the yoke of perpetual bondage,
or this were they willing to do. And
vhen they had besought the King on

this wise, he was moved unto tears
for very pity, and, agreeing unto the
petition, of the holy men, granted
them his pardon....

At the end of this time he invited
unto him all soever of most prowess
from far-off kingdoms and began to
multiply his household retinue, and
to hold such courtly fashion in his
household as begat rivalry amongst
peoples at a distance, insomuch as the
noblest in the land, fain to vie with him,
would hold himself as nought, save in
the cut of his clothes and the manner
of his arms he followed the pattern of
Arthur's knights. At last the fame of
his bounty and his prowess was upon
every man's tongue, even unto the
uttermost ends of the earth, and a fear
fell upon the Kings of realms oversea
lest he might fall upon them in arms
and they might lose the nations under
their dominion. Grievously tormented
of these devouring cares, they set them
to repairing their cities and the towers
of their cities, and builded them
strongholds in places meet for defence,
to the end that in case Arthur should
lead an expedition against them they
might find refuge therein should need
be. And when this was notified unto
Arthur, his heart was uplifted for that
he was a terror unto them all, and he set
his desire upon subduing the whole of
Europe unto himself. Fitting forth
his fleets accordingly, he made first of
all for Norway.

Geoffrey of Monmouth
Histories of the Kings of Britain
trans. Sebastian Evans, 1912

Marie de France – a critical vision

*French writers developed the Arthurian
legend later on. Marie de France's* Lai
de Lanval *revolves around the traditional*

*figures of the Arthurian legend, but
presents the royal couple in a negative
light. The hero of the lay is a knight from
Arthur's court whom Arthur 'forgets' when
the time comes for dispensing rewards and
fiefdoms. The queen tries to seduce Lanval,
and, when she fails, accuses him of
attempting to rape her; the king is furious
and imposes a sentence on the hero that
puts his life at risk.*

King Arthur – that fearless knight and
courteous lord – removed to Wales, and
lodged at Caerleon-on-Usk, since the
Picts and Scots did much mischief in
the land. For it was the wont of the wild
people of the north to enter in the realm
of Logres, and burn and damage at their
will. At the time of Pentecost, the king
cried a great feast. Thereat he gave many
rich gifts to his counts and barons, and
to the Knights of the Round Table.
Never were such worship and bounty
shown before at any feast, for Arthur
bestowed honours and lands on all his
servants – save only on one. This lord,
who was forgotten and misliked of the
king, was named Lanval....

Now it chanced, the same year, about
the feast of St John, a company of
knights came, for their solace, to an
orchard, beneath that tower where
dwelt the queen. Together with these
lords went Gawain and his cousin,
Yvain the fair....

Now the king that day had taken his
pleasure within the woods. He returned
from the chase towards evening, and
sought the chamber of the queen. When
the lady saw him, she sprang from her
bed, and kneeling at his feet, pleaded
for grace and pity. Lanval – she said
– had shamed her, since he required
her love....

Thereat the king waxed marvellously
wrathful, and swore a great oath that he

would set Lanval within a fire, or hang
him from a tree, if he could not deny
this thing, before his peers.

Marie de France
Old World Love Stories
trans. Eugene Mason, 191

The many faces of Arthur in the romances of Chrétien de Troyes

Erec et Enide, *the first of Chrétien de
Troyes' romances, opens with a scene that
was to become the traditional starting
point for the romances: Arthur's knights
assembled for a major Christian festival
(Ascension or Whitsun); the king himself,
wearing his crown, presiding over the
festivities; and an adventure that sets the
story in motion. In this case it is Arthur
himself who initiates the adventure –
during which Erec meets his destiny –
by proposing that they embark on a hunt
for the 'White Stag'. The whiteness of the
creature indicates that it is a supernatural
being and that the hunt will take Arthur's
knights on a journey into the Other
World. Gawain, more aware than his
companions of what is at stake, reproaches
the king for his rash resolve – but the die
has been cast....*

One Easter Day in the Springtime,
King Arthur held court in his town of
Cardigan. Never was there seen so rich
court; for many a good knight was there
hardy, bold, and brave, and rich ladies
and damsels, gentle and fair daughters
of kings. But before the court was
disbanded, the king told his knights that
he wished to hunt the White Stag, in
order to observe worthily the ancient
custom. When my lord Gawain heard
this, he was sore displeased, and said:
'Sire, you will derive neither thanks nor
goodwill from this hunt. We all know
long since what this custom of the
White Stag is: whoever can kill the

White Stag must forsooth kiss the fairest maiden of your court, come what may. But of this there might come great ill: for there are here five hundred damsels of high birth, gentle and prudent daughters of kings, and there is none of them but has a bold and valiant knight for her lover who would be ready to contend, whether right or wrong, that he who is his lady is the fairest and gentlest of them all.' The king replies: 'That I know well; yet will I not desist on that account; for a king's word ought never to be gainsaid. Tomorrow morning we shall all gaily go to hunt the White Stag in the forest of adventure. And very delightful this hunt will be.'

And so the affair is arranged for the next morning at daybreak. The morrow, as soon as it is day, the king gets up and dresses, and dons a short jacket for his forest ride. He commands the knights to be aroused and the horses to be made ready.

Chrétien de Troyes
Erec et Enide in *Arthurian Romances*,
trans. W. W. Comfort, 1914

The Arthur of Le Chevalier au lion *is a very different figure, whose wisdom and sense of justice are worthy of a great sovereign. Faced with a delicate matter concerning an inheritance, he is obliged to make a decision based on his own judgment, since the contest which was supposed to demonstrate 'the will of God' ended in a tie between Gawain and Yvain, the 'Chevalier au lion'.*

But the king ended the quarrel after he had listened to them a while; he had been pleased by what he had heard and so by the sight of their embrace of one another, although each had given the other many ugly wounds.

'My lords,' said Arthur, 'your great love for one another is manifest when each claims to have been defeated. But now rely on me, for I believe that I can effect a reconciliation that will bring honour to you both, and for which everyone will praise me.'

Then the two knights swore that they would do his will exactly as he stated it, and the king said that he would settle the dispute faithfully and justly.

'Where,' he said, 'is the damsel who has thrown her sister off her own land, and has forcibly and maliciously disinherited her?'

'Sire,' she said, 'here I am.'

'Are you there? Then come here! I have known for a long time that you were disinheriting her. Her rights will no longer be denied, for you yourself have just acknowledged the truth to me. It is right that you renounce all claims to her share.'

'Ah, my lord king! If I have given a foolish answer, you shouldn't hold me to my word! In God's name, sire, don't be hard on me! You are the king and should protect me from all wrong and error.'

'That is why,' said the king, 'I wish to restore to your sister her rightful share, for I have never wished to be party to any wrongdoing. And you have clearly heard that your knight and hers have submitted to my mercy. What I shall say may not please you, for your wrongdoing is well known. Each knight is so eager to honour the other that he claims to have been defeated. There is no need to delay further, since it has been left to me: either you will do everything I ask exactly as I state it, without deceit, or I will announce that my nephew has been defeated in battle. That would be much the worse for you, but I am prepared to say it against my inclination.'

In fact, he would never have said it at all, but he told her this to see whether he could frighten her so that she would restore her sister's inheritance to her out of fear, because he had clearly seen that only force or fear, and no amount of pleading, would ever convince her to restore it.

Because she was afraid and frightened, she said:

'Dear sir, I am compelled to do as you desire, but it grieves my heart. Yet I'll do it, though it hurts me: my sister will have what is rightfully her portion of my inheritance; I offer her you yourself as my pledge, so that she may be more assured of it.'

'Restore it to her at once,' said the king, 'and let her be your vassal woman and hold it from you; love her as your vassal woman and let her love you as her liege-lady and as her blood-related sister.'

Thus the king arranged the matter, and so the maiden was invested with her lands and thanked him for it. The king told his brave and valiant nephew to allow himself to be disarmed and asked my lord Yvain as well, if it pleased him, to have his armour removed, for they had no further need of it. Once the vassals had taken off their armour, they embraced one another as equals.

Chrétien de Troyes
The Knight with the Lion (Yvain)
in *Arthurian Romances*,
trans. William W. Kibler, 1991

Le Conte du Graal, *which was probably written around 1185, presents Arthur as a slightly ridiculous figure, incapable of defending himself against his enemies (and taking up the challenge when the red knight insults his wife), or even of imposing order in court. The young Perceval, who comes to his court hoping to*

Scene on the lid of an ivory casket showing Perceval arriving at Arthur's court.

be made a knight, is bitterly disappointed and goes to win his spurs elsewhere.

King Arthur was seated dejectedly at the head of a table; all the knights were eating and talking among themselves, except for Arthur who was disheartened and silent. The boy came forward but did not know whom to greet, since he did not recognize the king, until Yonet [Yvonet] came towards him holding a knife in his hand.

'Squire,' said the boy, 'you coming there with the knife in your hand, show me which of these men is the king.'

Yonet, who was very courteous, replied: 'Friend, there he is.'

The boy went to him at once and greeted him in his manner. The king was downcast and answered not a word so the boy spoke to him again. The king remained downcast and silent.

'By my faith,' the boy then said, 'this king never made a knight! How could he make knights if you can't get a word out of him?'

Immediately the boy prepared to depart; he turned his hunter's head but like the untutored fellow he was, he brought his horse so close to the king – I tell no lie – that he knocked the king's cap of fine cloth from his head on to the table.

The king turned his still-lowered head in the young man's direction, abandoned his serious thoughts, and said: 'Dear brother, welcome. I beg you not to take it ill that I failed to answer your greeting. My anger prevented a reply; for the greatest enemy I have, who hates and distresses me most, has just laid claim to my land and is so impertinent as to state that he'll have it whether I like it or not. He's called the Red Knight from the forest of Quinqueroy. And the queen had come here to sit in my presence, to see and to comfort these wounded knights. The knight would never have angered me by words alone, but he snatched away my cup and lifted it so insolently that he spilled all the wine in it over the queen. After this dreadful deed the queen returned to her chambers, in deadly fury and grief. So help me God, I don't think he'll come out alive.'

The boy did not give a fig for anything the king told him, nor did his grief or the shame done the queen make any impression on him.

'Make me a knight, sir king,' he said, 'for I wish to be on my way.'

The eyes of the rustic youth were bright and laughing in his head. None who saw him thought him wise, but everyone who observed him considered him handsome and noble.

'Friend,' said the king, 'dismount and give your hunter to this squire, who will watch over it and do whatever you ask. I swear to God that all will be done in accordance with my honour and to your benefit.'

And the boy replied: 'The knights I met in the heath never dismounted, yet you want me to dismount! By my head, I'll not dismount, so get on with it and I'll be on my way.'

'Ah!' said the king, 'my dear good friend, I'll willingly do it to your benefit and my honour.'

'By the faith I owe the Creator,' said the boy, 'good sir king, I'll never be a knight if I'm not a red knight. Grant me the armour of the knight I met outside your gate, the one who carried off your golden cup.'

The seneschal, who had been wounded, was angered by what he heard, and said: 'Right you are, friend! Go and snatch his armour from him right now, for it belongs to you. You were no fool to come here and ask for it!'

'Kay,' said the king, 'for the love of God, you are too eager to speak ill, and it doesn't matter to whom! This is a wicked vice in a gentleman. Though the boy is naive, still he may be of very noble line; and if his folly has come from poor teaching, because he had a low-bred master, he can still prove brave and wise. It is a wicked thing to mock another and to promise without giving. A gentleman should never undertake to promise anything to another that he cannot or will not grant him, for he might then earn the dislike of this person who otherwise would have been his friend but who, once the promise has been given, expects it to be kept. So by this you may understand that it is better to refuse a man something than to give him false hopes for, to tell the truth, he who makes promises he does not honour mocks and deceives himself, because it turns his friend's heart from him.' So the king spoke to Kay.

Chrétien de Troyes
The Story of the Grail (Perceval)
in *Arthurian Romances*,
trans. William W. Kibler, 1991

Arthur in the Middle Ages

The illustrious deeds of King Arthur and his knights were the subject matter of numerous romances written, first in verse and later in prose, from the second half of the 12th century and throughout the 13th.

Arthur fighting the Roman general Lucius (miniature from the *Roman de Brut*).

Arthur the general

In the oldest versions of the story Arthur was first and foremost a commander of armies, the dux bellorum *who succeeded in halting the Saxon advance and uniting the Britons against the invader. In the* Roman de Brut *by Wace (written in 1155), as in the* Historia Regum Britanniae *by Geoffrey of Monmouth, he is still the conquering hero who, not content merely to impose the* pax Arthuriana *in Logres, sails to the Continent to lead a victorious campaign against the Romans after they have wrongfully demanded tribute from Britain. In his reply, which is a model of classical rhetoric, Arthur proclaims the superiority of the Britons and, on the basis of certain historical precedents, goes so far as to assert Britain's rights over the Empire itself.*

'Consider first the case of Britain, and how to answer wisely therein. Britain was conquered by Caesar of force. The Britons knew not how to keep them against his host, and perforce paid him their tribute. But force is no right. It is but pride puffed up and swollen beyond measure. They cannot hold of law what they have seized by violence and wrong. The land is ours by right, even if the Roman took it to himself by force. The Romans really reproach us for the shame and the damage, the loss and the sorrow Caesar visited upon our fathers. They boast that they will avenge such losses as these, by taking the land with the rent, and making their little finger thicker than their father's loins. Let them beware. Hatred breeds hatred again, and things despiteful are done to those who despitefully use you. They come with threats, demanding truage, and reproving us for the evil we have done them. Tribute they claim by the right of the strong; leaving sorrow and shame as our portion. But if the Romans claim to receive tribute of Britain because tribute was aforetime paid them from Britain, by the same reasoning we may establish that Rome should rather pay tribute to us. In olden days, there lived two brothers, British born, namely, Belinus, King of the Britons, and Brennus, Duke of Burgundy, both wise and doughty lords. These stout champions arrived with their men before Rome, and shutting the city close, at the end gained it by storm. They took hostages of the citizens to pay them tribute; but since the burgesses did not observe their covenant, the brethren hanged the hostages, to the number of four-and-twenty, in the eyes of all their kinsfolk. When Belinus went to his own place, he commended Rome to the charge of Brennus, his brother. Now Constantine, the son of Helena, drew from Brennus and Belinus, and in his turn held Rome in his care. Maximian, King of Britain, after he had conquered France and Germany, passed the Mont St Bernard into Lombardy, and took Rome to his keeping. These mighty kings were my near kinsmen, and each was master of Rome. Thus you have heard, and see clearly, that not only am I King of Britain, but by law Emperor of Rome also, so we maintain the rights of our fathers. The Romans have had truage of us, and my ancestors have taken seisin of them. They claim Britain, and I demand Rome. This is the sum and end of my counsel as regards Britain and Rome. Let him have the fief and the rent who is mightier in the field. As to France and those other countries which have been removed from their hands, the Romans should not wish to possess that which they may not maintain. Either the land was not to

their mind, or they had not the strength to hold it. Perchance the Romans have no rights in the matter, and it is by reason of covetousness rather than by love of law, that they seek this quarrel. Let him keep the land who can, by the right of the most strong. For all these things the emperor menaces us very grievously. I pray God that he may do us no harm. Our fiefs and goods he promises to take from us, and lead us captive in bonds to Rome. We care not overmuch for this, and are not greatly frighted at his words. If he seek us after his boast, please God, he will have no mind to threaten when he turns again to his own home. We accept his challenge, and appeal to God's judgment, that all may be rendered to his keeping, who is able to maintain it in his hand.'

Wace
Roman de Brut in *Arthurian Chronicles*
trans. Eugene Mason, 1912

And legendary hero

As the commander-in-chief who led Britain's army against Rome, Arthur was responsible for organizing military divisions and strategy, but he played no part in the actual combat: he was the rex otiosus, *guarantor of the royal office. But the king had a heroic past, traces of which were still to be found in the 12th- and 13th-century texts, one example being the account of his battle with the giant of Mont-Saint-Michel. The giant had abducted the daughter of Arthur's loyal vassal Duke Hoël of Brittany and had killed the girl while raping her.*

Arthur, Bedevere, and Kay, the three together, began briskly to climb the mount. After they had climbed for a while Arthur spake to his fellows: 'Comrades, I go before to do battle with the giant. For your part you must follow a little after. But let neither of you be so bold as to aid me in my quarrel, so long as I have strength to strive. Be the buffets what they may, stand you still, unless he beats me to the ground. It is not seemly that any, save one, should have lot in this business. Nevertheless so you see me in utmost peril and fear, come swiftly to my succour, nor let me find death at his hands.' Sir Kay and Sir Bedevere made this covenant with their lord, and the three knights together set forth again up the hill. Now when Arthur drew near to the summit of the mount, he beheld the giant crouched above his fire. He broiled a hog within the flame upon a spit. Part of the flesh he had eaten already, and part of the meat was charred and burning in the fire. He was the more hideous to see because his beard and hair were foul with blood and coal. Arthur trusted to take him thus unready, before he could get to his mace. But the giant spied his adversary, and all amarvelled leapt lightly on his feet. He raised the club above his shoulder, albeit so heavy that no two peasants of the country could lift it from the ground. Arthur saw the giant afoot, and the blow about to fall. He gripped his sword, dressing the buckler high to guard his head. The giant struck with all his strength upon the shield, so that the mountain rang like an anvil. The stroke was stark, and Arthur stood mazed at the blow, but he was hardy and strong, and did not reel. When the king came to himself, and marked the shield shattered on his arm, he was marvellously wroth. He raised his sword and struck full at the giant's brow. The blow was shrewd, and would have brought the combat to an end had not the giant parried with his mace. Even so, his head was sorely hurt, and the blood ran down his face, that he might not see. When the giant knew that he was wounded to his hurt, he became in his rage as a beast possessed. He turned grimly on his adversary, even as the boar, torn of the hounds and mangled by the hunting knife, turns on the hunter. Filled with ire and malice the giant rushed blindly on the king. Heedless of the sword, he flung his arms about him, and putting forth the full measure of his might, bore Arthur to his knees. Arthur was ardent and swift and ready of wit. He remembered his manhood, and struggled upright on his feet. He was altogether angered, and fearful of what might hap. Since strength could not help, he called subtlety to his aid. Arthur made his body stiff like a rod, and held himself close, for he was passing strong. He feigned to spring on his foe, but turning aside, slipped quickly from under the giant's arms. When Arthur knew his person free of these bands, he passed swiftly to and fro, eluding his enemy's clasp. Now he was here, now there, ofttimes striking with the sword. The giant ran blindly about, groping with his hands, for his eyes were full of blood, and he knew not white from black. Sometimes Arthur was before him, sometimes behind, but never in his grip; till at the end the king smote him so fiercely with Excalibur that the blade clove to his brain, and he fell. He cried out in his pain, and the noise of his fall and of this exceeding bitter cry was as fetters of iron tormented by the storm.

Arthur stood a little apart, and gazed upon his adversary. He laughed aloud in his mirth; for his anger was well-nigh gone. He commanded Bedevere, his cupbearer, to strike off the giant's head, and deliver it to the squires, that they might bear it to the host, for the greater marvel. Bedevere did after his

A rthur fights the giant on Mont-Saint-
Michel.

lord's behest. He drew his sword, and
divided the head from the shoulders.
Wonderfully huge and hideous to sight
was the head of this giant. Never, said
Arthur, had he known such fear; neither
had met so perilous a giant, save only
that Riton, who had grieved so many
fair kings. This Riton in his day made
war upon divers kings. Of these some
were slain in battle, and others remained
captive in his hand. Alive or dead, Riton
used them despitefully; for it was his
wont to shave the beards of these kings,
and purfle therewith a cloak of furs that
he wore, very rich. Vainglorious beyond
measure was Riton of his broidered
cloak. Now by reason of folly and
lightness, Riton sent messages to Arthur,
bidding him shave his beard, and
commend it forthwith to the giant,
in all good will. Since Arthur was a
mightier lord and a more virtuous
prince than his fellows, Riton made
covenant to prefer his beard before

theirs, and hold it in honour as the most
silken fringe of his mantle. Should
Arthur refuse to grant Riton the trophy,
then nought was there to do, but that
body to body they must fight out their
quarrel, in single combat, alone. He who
might slay his adversary, or force him to
own himself vanquished, should have
the beard for his guerdon, together with
the mantle of furs, fringes and garniture
and all. Arthur accorded with the giant
that this should be so. They met in
battle on a high place, called Mount
Aravius, in the far east, and there the
king slew Riton with the sword, spoiling
him of that rich garment of furs, with its
border of dead kings' beards. Therefore,
said Arthur, that never since that day
had he striven with so perilous a giant,
nor with one of whom he was so sorely
frighted. Nevertheless Dinabuc was
bigger and mightier than was Riton,
even in the prime of his youth and
strength. For a monster more loathly
and horrible, a giant so hideous and
misshapen, was never slain by man,
than the devil Arthur killed to himself
that day, in Mont St Michel, over
against the sea.

After Arthur had slain the monster,
and Bedevere had taken his head, they
went their way to the host in great mirth
and content. They reached the camp,
and showed the spoil to all who would,
for their hearts were high with that
which they had done.

Wace, *Roman de Brut*, in *Arthurian
Chronicles*, trans. Eugene Mason, 1912

Arthur the man of action

Layamon, who wrote the Brut *around
1200, developed the Arthurian legend
by adding to its magical qualities.*

There Uther the king took Ygaerne for
queen; Ygaerne was with child by Uther

the king, all through Merlin's craft, before she was wedded. The time came that was chosen, then was Arthur born. So soon as he came on earth, elves took him; they enchanted the child with magic most strong, they gave him might to be the best of all knights; they gave him another thing, that he should be a rich king; they gave him the third, that he should live long; they gave to him the prince virtues most good, so that he was most generous of all men alive. This the elves gave him, and thus the child thrived....

When Arthur was king – hearken now a marvellous thing; – he was liberal to each man alive, knight with the best, wondrously keen! He was to the young for father, to the old for comforter, and with the unwise wonderfully stern; wrong was to him exceeding loathsome, and the right ever dear. Each of his cupbearers, and of his chamber-thanes, and his chamber-knights, bare gold in hand, to back and to bed, clad with gold web. He had never any cook, that he was not champion most good; never any knight's swain, that he was not bold thane! The king held all his folk together with great bliss; and with such things he overcame all kings, with fierce strength and with treasure. Such were his qualities, that all folk it knew. Now was Arthur good king; his people loved him; eke it was known wide, of his kingdom....

Arthur marched to Cornwall, with an immense army. Modred heard that, and advanced against him with innumerable folk – there were many fated! Upon the Tambre they came together; the place hight Camelford, evermore lasted the same word. And at Camelford was assembled sixty thousand men, and more thousands thereto; Modred was their chief. Then thitherward gan ride

Arthur the mighty, with innumerable folk – fated though it were! Upon the Tambre they encountered together; elevated their standards; advanced together; drew their long swords, and smote on the helms; fire out sprang; spears splintered; shields gan shiver; shafts brake in pieces! There fought all together innumerable folk! Tambre was in flood with blood to excess; there might no man in the fight know any warrior, nor who did worse, nor who did better, so was the conflict mingled! For each slew downright, were he swain, were he knight. There was Modred slain, and deprived of life-day, and all his knights slain in the fight. There were slain all the brave, Arthur's warriors, high and low, and all the Britons of Arthur's board, and all his dependants, of many kingdoms. And Arthur himself wounded with a broad slaughter-spear; fifteen dreadful wounds he had; in the least one might thrust two gloves! Then was there no more remained in the fight, of two hundred thousand men that there lay hewed in pieces, except Arthur the king alone, and two of his knights.

Arthur was wounded wondrously much. There came to him a lad, who was of his kindred; he was Cador's son, the Earl of Cornwall; Constantine the lad hight, he was dear to the king. Arthur looked on him, where he lay on the ground, and said these words, with sorrowful heart: 'Constantine, thou art welcome; thou wert Cador's son. I give thee here my kingdom, and defend thou my Britons ever in thy life, and maintain them all the laws that have stood in my days, and all the good laws that in Uther's days stood. And I will fare to Avalun, to the fairest of all maidens, to Argante the queen, an elf most fair, and she shall make my wounds all sound; make me all whole with healing draughts. And afterwards I will come again to my kingdom, and dwell with the Britons with mickle joy.'

Even with the words there approached from the sea that was a short boat, floating with the waves; and two women therein, wondrously formed; and they took Arthur anon, and bare him quickly, and laid him softly down, and forth they gan depart.

Then was it accomplished that Merlin whilom said, that mickle care should be of Arthur's departure. The Britons believe yet that he is alive, and dwelleth in Avalun with the fairest of all elves; and the Britons ever yet expect when Arthur shall return. Was never the man born, of ever any lady chosen, that knoweth of the sooth, to say more of Arthur. But whilom was a sage hight Merlin; he said with words – his sayings were sooth – that an Arthur should yet come to help the English.

Layamon
Brut in Wace and Layamon
Arthurian Chronicles
trans. Eugene Mason, 1912

Of Arthour and of Merlin

The romance Of Arthour and of Merlin *is a 'translation' – or rather a free adaptation – of the French romance* Merlin, *attributed to Robert de Boron. In the following passage, the young Arthur is knighted by his foster father (a detail omitted by the French versions) before being acknowledged as king because he has been able to draw the sword out of the stone (pictured right).*

Antor came forward immediately and knighted Arthur on the spot; first he procured him harness and coverlet, then steed and saddle, helm and mailshirt and halbergam, thigh-covering gaiters and leather doublet, a square shield, a good sword of steel, and a hard well-biting lance. Then right away he gave him forty knights to serve him. Next day they went to a tournament, and there indeed they behaved so that every day Sir Arthur won the prize and the praise. The next day Antor, who was not negligent, went to Bishop Brice and told him he knew a knight, both high-born and noble, 'who should be our king by right, for he can draw out this sword'.

The bishop was very happy, and he sent for Arthur at once; in front of all the high and mighty of the country, Arthur took the sword in his hand. He drew it and thrust it out. Many men wondered much, because nobody had been able to move it, except for him – I warrant it to you. Kings and earls, of a certainty, they all started immediately to discuss with him, in order to put him to the test. But he remained of good cheer, and they themselves could not have devised wiser answers than the ones he gave them. Sir Antor helped him so that he was then chosen as king. And many princes and many knights were invited to the feast of his coronation: all those who would come should be present on St John's Feast.

The Round Table and the Holy Grail

At the very end of the Middle Ages, Arthurian literature culminated in three English masterpieces, Sir Gawain and the Green Knight *(pre-1400), Sir Thomas Malory's* Le Morte d'Arthur *(finished 1470; published 1485) and Edmund Spenser's* Faerie Queene *(1596).* Sir Gawain *is one of the first literary texts of fiction to be written in English. Malory's work combines and summarizes a whole range of French sources into a connected narrative rich in human interest and pathos. Spenser's use of the legend is more allusive and the figure of Arthur (in the six cantos out of the twelve, which were all he lived to complete) appears only sporadically.*

Sir Gawain and the Green Knight (pre-1400) is the most famous Arthurian romance of the English Middle Ages; it contrasts the splendour of King Arthur's court with the danger of the mysterious outside world, which Gawain will have to enter in order to fulfil a rash promise.

But of all who abode here of Britain's kings,
Arthur was highest in honour, as I have heard;
So I intend to tell you of a true wonder,
Which many folk mention as a manifest marvel,
A happening eminent among Arthur's adventures.
Listen to my lay but a little while:
Straightway shall I speak it, in city as I heard it,
With tongue;
As scribes have set it duly
In the lore of the land so long,
With letters linking truly
In story bold and strong.

This king lay at Camelot one Christmastide
With many mighty lords, manly liegemen,
Members rightly reckoned of the Round Table,
In splendid celebration, seemly and carefree.
There tussling in tournament time and again
Jousted in jollity these gentle knights,
Then in court carnival sang catches and danced;
For fifteen days the feasting there was full in like measure
With all the meat and merry-making men could devise,
Gladly ringing glee, glorious to hear,
A noble din by day, dancing at night!
All was happiness in the height in halls

and chambers
For lords and their ladies, delectable joy.
With all delights on earth they housed
    there together,
Saving Christ's self, the most celebrated
    knights,
The loveliest ladies to live in all time,
And the comeliest king ever to keep
    court.
For this fine fellowship was in its fair
    prime
Far famed,
Stood well in heaven's will,
Its high-souled king acclaimed:
So hardy a host on hill
Could not with ease be named.
>   *Sir Gawain and the Green Knight*
>   trans. Brian Stone, 1974

Marriage and the Round Table

*Malory connects the acquisition of the
Round Table with Arthur's marriage
to Guinevere.*

So it fell on a time King Arthur said
unto Merlin, 'My barons will let me
have no rest, but needs I must take a
wife, and I will none take but by thy
counsel and by thine advice.'

'It is well done,' said Merlin, 'that ye
take a wife, for a man of your bounty
and noblesse should not be without a
wife. Now is there any that ye love more
than another?'

'Yea,' said King Arthur, 'I love
Guenever the King's daughter
Leodegrance, of the land of Camelerd,
he which holdeth in his house the
Table Round that ye told he had of my
father Uther. And this damosel is the
most valiant and fairest lady that I know
living, or yet that ever I could find.'

'Sir,' said Merlin, 'as of her beauty
and fairness she is one of the fairest
live, but and ye loved her not so well as
e do, I should find you a damosel of

beauty and of goodness that should like
you and please you, and your heart were
not set; but there as a man's heart is set,
he will be loth to return.'

'That is truth,' said King Arthur.

But Merlin warned the king covertly
that Guenever was not wholesome for
him to take to wife, for he warned him
that Launcelot should love her, and she
him again; and so he turned his tale to
the adventures of Sangrail. Then Merlin
desired of the king for to have men with
him that should enquire of Guenever,
and so the king granted him, and
Merlin went forth unto King
Leodegrance of Camelerd, and told him
of the desire of the king that he would
have unto his wife Guenever his
daughter.

'That is to me,' said King
Leodegrance, 'the best tidings that ever
I heard, that so worthy a king of prowess
and noblesse will wed my daughter.
And as for my lands, I will give him,
wist I it might please him, but he hath
lands enow, him needeth none, but I
shall send him a gift shall please him
much more, for I shall give him the
Table Round, the which Uther
Pendragon gave me, and when it is full
complete, there is an hundred knights
and fifty. And as for an hundred good
knights I have myself, but I fault fifty,
for so many have been slain in my days.'

And so Leodegrance delivered his
daughter Guenever unto Merlin, and
the Table Round with the hundred
knights, and so they rode freshly, with
great royalty, what by water and what
by land, till they came nigh unto
London....

When King Arthur heard of the
coming of Guenever and the hundred
knights with the Table Round, then
King Arthur made great joy for her
coming, and that rich present, and said

openly, 'This fair lady is passing
welcome unto me, for I have loved her
long, and therefore there is nothing so
leve to me. And these knights with the
Round Table please me more than right
great riches.'

And in all haste the king let ordain
for the marriage and the coronation in
the most honourable wise that could be
devised. 'Now, Merlin,' said King
Arthur, 'go thou and espy me in all this
land fifty knights which be of most
prowess and worship.'

Within short time Merlin had found
such knights that should fulfil twenty
and eight knights, but no more he could
find. Then the Bishop of Canterbury
was fetched, and he blessed the sieges
with great royalty and devotion, and
there set the eight and twenty knights in
their sieges.

And when this was done Merlin said,
'Fair sirs, you must all arise and come to
King Arthur for to do him homage; he
will have the better will to maintain
you.'

And so they arose and did their
homage, and when they were gone
Merlin found in every sieges letters of
gold that told the knights' names that
had sitten therein. But two sieges were
void.

And so anon came young Gawain and
asked the king a gift.

'Ask,' said the king, 'and I shall grant
it you.'

'Sir, I ask that ye will make me knight
that same day ye shall wed fair
Guenever.'

'I will do it with a good will,' said
King Arthur, 'and do unto you all the
worship that I may, for I must by reason
ye are mine nephew, my sister's son.'

Thomas Malory
Le Morte d'Arthur, Vol. I, Book III,
Chapters 1 and 2, 1485

The perfect knight

Spenser describes Arthur in Book I of The
Faerie Queene, *but does not name him.*

At last she chaunced by good hap to
meet
A goodly knight, faire marching by the
way
Together with his Squire, arayed meet:
His glitterand armour shined farre away,
Like glauncing light of *Phoebus* brightest
ray;
From top to toe no place appeared bare,
That deadly dint of steele endanger may:
Athwart his brest a bauldrick braue he
warĕ,
That shynd, like twinkling stars, with
stons most pretious rare.

And in the midst thereof one pretious
stone
Of wondrous worth, and eke of
wondrous mights,
Shapt like a Ladies head, exceeding
shone,
Like *Hesperus* emongst the lesser lights,
And stroue for to amaze the weaker
sights;
Thereby his mortall blade full comely
hong
In yuory sheath, ycaru'd with curious
slights;
Whose hilts were burnisht gold, and
handle strong
Of mother pearle, and buckled with a
golden tong.

His haughtie helmet, horrid all with
gold,
Both glorious brightnesse, and great
terrour bred;
For all the crest a Dragon did enfold
With greedie pawes, and ouer all did
spred
His golden wings: his dreadfull hideous
hed
Close couched on the beuer, seem'd

to throw
From flaming mouth bright sparkles
    fierie red,
That suddeine horror to faint harts did
    show;
And scaly tayle was stretcht adowne his
    backe full low.

Vpon the top of all his loftie crest,
A bunch of haires discolourd diuersly,
With sprincled pearle, and gold full
    richly drest,
Did shake, and seem'd to daunce for
    iollity,
Like to an Almond tree ymounted hye
On top of greene *Selinis* all alone,
With blossomes braue bedecked
    daintily;
Whose tender locks do tremble euery
    one
At euery little breath, that vnder heauen
    is blowne.

His warlike shield all closely couer'd
    was,
Ne might of mortall eye be euer seene;
Not made of steele, nor of enduring
    bras,
Such earthly mettals soone consumed
    bene:
But all of Diamond perfect pure and
    cleene
It framed was, one massie entire mould,
Hewen out of Adamant rocke with
    engines keene,
That point of speare it neuer percen
    could,
Ne dint of direfull sword diuide the
    substance would.

The same to wight he neuer wont
    disclose,
But when as monsters huge he would
    dismay,
Or daunt vnequall armies of his foes,
Or when the flying heauens he would

affray;
For so exceeding shone his glistring ray,
That *Phoebus* golden face it did attaint,
As when a cloud his beames doth ouer-
    lay;
And siluer *Cynthia* wexed pale and faint,
As when her face is staynd with magicke
    arts constraint.

No magicke arts hereof had any might,
Nor bloudie wordes of bold
    Enchaunters call,
But all that was not such, as seemd in
    sight,
Before that shield did fade, and
    suddeine fall:
And when him list the raskall routes
    appall,
Men into stones therewith he could
    transmew,
And stones to dust, and dust to nought
    at all;
And when him list the prouder lookes
    subdew,
He would them gazing blind, or turne
    to other hew.

Ne let it seeme, that credence this
    exceedes,
For he that made the same, was knowne
    right well
To haue done much more admirable
    deedes.
It *Merlin* was, which whylome did excell
All liuing wightes in might of magicke
    spell:
Both shield, and sword, and armour all
    he wrought
For this young Prince, when first to
    armes he fell;
But when he dyde, the Faerie Queene it
    brought
To Faerie lond, where yet it may be
    seen, if sought.

Edmund Spenser, *The Faerie Queene*
Book I, Canto vii, 1596

Arthur in the 19th and 20th centuries

The Arthurian epic held little interest for the Hanoverians, and with the advent of the 18th century – and the Age of Reason – Arthur was largely forgotten by the English-speaking world. Nineteenth-century art, and in particular literature, witnessed a revival of interest in the legend that has persisted to some extent ever since.

The 19th century: Tennyson and the Pre-Raphaelites

It is largely to the poet Alfred, Lord Tennyson (1809–92), that we owe the rediscovery of the legend in the 19th century. Tennyson, who was to become Poet Laureate in 1850, published a first sequence of poems for Idylls of the King *in 1859; another sequence followed in 1869. Written in a romantic style that corresponded to Pre-Raphaelite tastes in painting, these poems cover all the major episodes from the legend and have proved unfailingly popular. Pre-Raphaelite painters like Burne-Jones and Rossetti illustrated some of the most famous scenes from them and successive writers have continued to draw inspiration from the Arthurian theme. Tennyson's 'Lady of Shalott', which tells the moving story of a young woman who dies of unrequited love for Lancelot, is a classical text which is still studied in schools, and for many young students it provides their first contact with the legend of King Arthur.*

His broad clear brow in sunlight glow'd;
On burnish'd hooves his war-horse
    trode;
From underneath his helmet flow'd
His coal-black curls as on he rode,
    As he rode down to Camelot.
From the bank and from the river
He flash'd into the crystal mirror,
'Tirra lirra,' by the river
        Sang Sir Lancelot.

She left the web, she left the loom,
She made three paces thro' the room,
She saw the water-lily bloom,
She saw the helmet and the plume,
    She look'd down to Camelot.
Out flew the web and floated wide;

Engraving by Dante Gabriel Rossetti entitled *The Lady of Shalott.*

The mirror crack'd from side to side;
'The curse is come upon me,' cried
    The Lady of Shalott....

And down the river's dim expanse
Like some bold seer in a trance,
Seeing all his own mischance –
With a glassy countenance
    Did she look to Camelot.
And at the closing of the day
She loosed the chain, and down she lay;
The broad stream bore her far away,
    The Lady of Shalott.

Lying, robed in snowy white
That loosely flew to left and right –
The leaves upon her falling light –
Thro' the noises of the night
    She floated down to Camelot:
And as the boat-head wound along
The willowy hills and fields among,
They heard her singing her last song,
    The Lady of Shalott.
        Alfred, Lord Tennyson,
        'The Lady of Shalott',
        Idylls of the King, 1869

Tennyson's Idylls of the King *gives us the Arthurian story at its most romantic. When the king is dying he bids Sir Bedevere return Excalibur to the waters of the lake from which he had received it. Twice Sir Bedevere goes to the lakeside, but, bewitched by the sword's splendour, he cannot bring himself to throw it in, telling Arthur:*

'I heard the water lapping on the crag,
And the long ripple washing in the
   reeds.'

Arthur knows he is lying and bids him go a third time.

Then quickly rose Sir Bedevere, and ran,
And, leaping down the ridges lightly,
   plunged
Among the bulrush beds, and clutch'd

the sword,
And strongly wheel'd and threw it. The
   great brand
Made lightnings in the splendour of the
   moon,
And flashing round and round, and
   whirl'd in an arch,
Shot like a streamer of the northern
   morn,
Seen where the moving isles of winter
   shock
By night, with noises of the Northern
   Sea.
So flash'd and fell the brand Excalibur:
But ere he dipt the surface, rose an arm
Clothed in white samite, mystic,
   wonderful,
And caught him by the hilt, and
   brandish'd him
Three times, and drew him under in the
   mere.
And lightly went the other to the King.

Then spoke King Arthur, drawing
   thicker breath:
'Now see I by thine eyes that this is
   done.
Speak out: what is it thou hast heard, or
   seen?'

And answer made the bold Sir Bedivere:
'Sir King, I closed mine eyelids, lest the
   gems
Should blind my purpose, for I never
   saw,
Nor shall see, here or elsewhere, till I
   die,
Not tho' I live three lives of mortal men,
So great a miracle as yonder hilt.
Then with both hands I flung him,
   wheeling him;
But when I look'd again, behold an arm,
Clothed in white samite, mystic,
   wonderful,
That caught him by the hilt, and
   brandish'd him

Three times, and drew him under in the
  mere.'

And answer made King Arthur,
  breathing hard:
'My end draws nigh; 'tis time that I
  were gone.
Make broad thy shoulders to receive my
  weight,
And bear me to the margin; yet I fear
My wound hath taken cold, and I shall
  die.'

Alfred, Lord Tennyson
'The Passing of Arthur'
Idylls of the King, 1869

*A recurrent theme at the end of the
century was the seduction of Merlin by the
Lady of the Lake, the subtle enchantress
Nimue, or Viviane – for 19th-century
Victorian society the embodiment of the
dangerous femme fatale. At the same time
a number of texts broached the question
of Guinevere's culpability in betraying
Arthur for Lancelot, and the degree to
which she could be held responsible for the
final catastrophe. William Morris'*
Defence of Guinevere, *for example,
enjoyed a brief hour of glory, but the
majority of these texts are forgotten today,
and with good reason. Their abundance,
however, demonstrates the unvarying
popularity of Arthurian subject matter
between 1840 and 1900.*

William Morris, *The Defence of Guinevere*

*Accused, Guinevere defends herself in
front of Gauwaine, once her friend, now
her most aggressive accuser. She does it
paradoxically, remembering the main steps
of her tragic affair with Lancelot, and at
the same time claiming she is innocent.*

No minute of the wild day ever slips
From out my memory; I hear thrushes
  sing,

And wheresoever I may be, straightway
Thoughts of it all come up with most
  fresh sting:
I was half mad with beauty on that day,
And went without my ladies all alone,
In a quiet garden walled round every
  way;
I was right joyful of that wall of stone,
That shut the flowers and trees up with
  the sky,
And trebled all the beauty: to the bone,
Yea right through to my heart, grown
  very shy
With weary thoughts, it pierced, and
  made me glad;
Exceedingly glad, and I knew verily,
A little thing just then had made me
  mad;
I dared not think, as I was wont to do,
Sometimes, upon my beauty; if I had
Held out my long hand up against the
  blue,
And, looking on the tenderly darken'd
  fingers,
Thought that by rights one ought to see
  quite through,
There, see you, where the soft still light
  yet lingers,
Round by the edges; what should I have
  done,
If this had joined with yellow spotted
  singers,
And startling green drawn upward by
  the sun?
But shouting, loosed out, see now! all
  my hair,
And trancedly stood watching the west
  wind run
With faintest half-heard breathing
  sound: why there
I lose my head e'en now in doing this;
But shortly listen: In that garden fair
Came Launcelot walking; this is true,
  the kiss
Wherewith we kissed in meeting that
  spring day,

scarce dare talk of the remember'd
bliss,
When both our mouths went wandering
in one way,
And aching sorely, met among the
leaves;
Our hands being left behind strained far
away.
Never within a yard of my bright sleeves
Had Launcelot come before: and now so
nigh!
After that day why is it Guinevere
grieves?
Nevertheless you, O Sir Gauwaine, lie,
Whatever happened on through all
those years,
God knows I speak truth, saying that
you lie.
Being such a lady could I weep these
tears
If this were true? A great queen such as I
Having sinn'd this way, straight her
conscience sears;
And afterwards she liveth hatefully,
Slaying and poisoning, certes never
weeps:
Gauwaine be friends now, speak me
lovingly.
Do I not see how God's dear pity creeps
All through your frame, and trembles in
your mouth?
Remember in what grave your mother
sleeps,
Buried in some place far down in the
south,
Men are forgetting as I speak to you;
By her head sever'd in that awful drouth
Of pity that drew Agravaine's fell blow,
I pray you pity! let me not scream out
For ever after, when the shrill winds
blow
Through half your castle-locks! let me
not shout
For ever after in the winter night
When you ride out alone! in battle-rout
Let not my rusting tears make your

sword light!
Ah! God of mercy, how he turns away!
So, ever must I dress me to the fight,
So: let God's justice work!

William Morris
The Defence of Guinevere, 1858

Mark Twain

*By the end of the century the Arthurian
legend was sufficiently integrated into the
cultural heritage for an American writer
like Mark Twain to write* A Connecticut
Yankee in King Arthur's Court *(1889),
one of the earliest works of science fiction
using the theme of time travel. Its young
hero, Hank Morgan, travels back in time
to Arthur's court and helps the ineffectual
king triumph over his enemies. Despite
its scant respect for historical details,* A
Connecticut Yankee *demonstrates the
important place occupied by the Arthurian
legend in the Anglo-Saxon imagination.*

*Mark Twain's purpose in writing the
novel was 'to group together some of the
most odious laws which have had vogue
in the Christian countries within the past
eight or ten centuries, and illustrate them
by the incidents of a story' and to lay bare
'the blank and sterile ignorance of that
day and contrast it with the vast and
many-sided knowledge of this'. Here
Hank, a foreman in a Connecticut gun
factory, describes his first sight of Arthur's
court and his introduction to the art
of the tourney.*

In the middle of this groined and
vaulted public square was an oaken table
which they called the Table Round. It
was as large as a circus ring; and around
it sat a great company of men dressed in
such various and splendid colors that it
hurt one's eyes to look at them. They
wore their plumed hats, right along,
except that whenever one addressed
himself directly to the king, he lifted his

hat a trifle just as he was beginning his remark.

Mainly they were drinking – from entire ox horns; but a few were still munching bread or gnawing beef bones. There was about an average of two dogs to one man; and these sat in expectant attitudes till a spent bone was flung to them, and then they went for it by brigades and divisions, with a rush, and there ensued a fight which filled the prospect with a tumultuous chaos of plunging heads and bodies and flashing tails, and the storm of howlings and barkings deafened all speech for the time; but that was no matter, for the dog-fight was always a bigger interest anyway; the men rose, sometimes, to observe it the better and bet on it, and the ladies and the musicians stretched themselves out over their balusters with the same object; and all broke into delighted ejaculations from time to time. In the end, the winning dog stretched himself out comfortably with his bone between his paws, and proceeded to growl over it, and gnaw it, and grease the floor with it, just as fifty others were already doing; and the rest of the court resumed their previous industries and entertainments.

As a rule the speech and behavior of these people were gracious and courtly; and I noticed that they were good and serious listeners when anybody was telling anything – I mean in a dog-fightless interval. And plainly, too, they were a childlike and innocent lot; telling lies of the stateliest pattern with a most gentle and winning naivety, and ready and willing to listen to anybody else's lie, and believe it, too. It was hard to associate them with anything cruel or dreadful; and yet they dealt in tales of blood and suffering with a guileless relish that

made me almost forget to shudder....

Mainly the Round Table talk was monologues – narrative accounts of the adventures in which these prisoners were captured and their friends and backers killed and stripped of their steeds and armor. As a general thing – as far as I could make out – these murderous adventures were not forays undertaken to avenge injuries, nor to settle old disputes or sudden fallings out; no, as a rule they were simply duels between strangers – duels between people who had never even been introduced to each other, and between whom existed no cause of offense whatever. Many a time I had seen a couple of boys, strangers, meet by chance, and say simultaneously 'I can lick you', and go at it on the spot; but I had always imagined until now, that that sort of thing belonged to children only, and was a sign and mark of childhood; but here were these big boobies sticking to it and taking pride in it clear up into full age and beyond. Yet there was something very engaging about these great simple-hearted creatures, something attractive and lovable. There did not seem to be brains enough in the entire nursery, so to speak, to bait a fish-hook with; but you didn't seem to mind that, after a little, because you soon saw that brains were not needed in a society like that, and, indeed would have marred it, hindered it, spoiled its symmetry – perhaps rendered its existence impossible....

We had one tournament which was continued from day to day during more than a week, and as many as five hundred knights took part in it, from first to last. They were weeks gathering. They came on horseback from everywhere; from the very ends of the country, and even from beyond the sea; and many brought ladies and all brought squires, and troops of servants. It was a most gaudy and gorgeous crowd, as to costumery, and very characteristic of the country and the time, in the way of high animal spirits, innocent indecencies of language, and happy-hearted indifference to morals. It was fight or look on, all day and every day; and sing, gamble, dance, carouse, half the night every night. They had a most noble good time. You never saw such people. Those banks of beautiful ladies, shining in their barbaric splendors, would see a knight sprawl from his horse in the lists with a lance-shaft the thickness of your ankle clean through him and the blood spouting, and instead of fainting they would clap their hands and crowd each other for a better view; only sometimes one would dive into her handkerchief, and look ostentatiously broken-hearted, and then you could lay two to one that there was a scandal there somewhere and she was afraid the public hadn't found it out.

Mark Twain, *A Connecticut Yankee in King Arthur's Court*, 1889

The 20th century: E. A. Robinson, *Lancelot*

The importance of the legend was consolidated in the 20th century. This passage comes at the end of Section V, after the discovery of Lancelot and Guinevere in bed together. King Arthur has commanded that the queen be burnt on a pyre, and Lancelot has rescued her, but in so doing has by mischance killed Gawaine's youngest brother, shattering all hope of a future reconciliation.

The King, alone with Gawaine, who
    said nothing,
Had yet no heart for news of Lancelot
Or Guinevere. He saw them on their
    way

To Joyous Gard, where Tristram and
    Isolt
Had islanded of old their stolen love,
While Mark of Cornwall entertained a
    vengeance
Envisaging an ending of all that;
And he could see the two of them
    together
As Mark had seen Isolt there, and her
    knight, –
Though not, like Mark, with murder in
    his eyes.
He saw them as if they were there
    already,
And he were a lost thought long out of
    mind;
He saw them lying in each other's arms,
Oblivious of the living and the dead
They left in Camelot. Then he saw the
    dead
That lay so quiet outside the city walls,
And wept, and left the Queen to
    Lancelot –
Or would have left her, had the will
    been his
To leave or take; for now he could
    acknowledge
An inrush of a desolate thanksgiving
That she, with death around her, had
    not died.
The vision of a peace that humbled him,
And yet might save the world that he
    had won,
Came slowly into view like something
    soft
And ominous on all-fours, without a
    spirit
To make it stand upright. 'Better be
    that,
Even that, than blood,' he sighed, 'if
    that be peace.'
But looking down on Gawaine, who
    said nothing,
He shook his head: 'The King has had
    his world,
And he shall have no peace. With

Modred here,
And Agravaine with Gareth, who is dead
With Gaheris, Gawaine will have no
    peace.
Gawaine or Modred – Gawaine with his
    hate,
Or Modred with his anger for his birth,
And the black malady of his ambition –
Will make of my Round Table, where
    was drawn
The circle of a world, a thing of wreck
And yesterday – a furniture forgotten;
And I, who loved the world as Merlin
    did,
May lose it as he lost it, for a love
That was not peace, and therefore was
    not love.'

        E. A. Robinson, *Lancelot*, 1920,
          in *Arthurian Poets*, 1990

Jean Cocteau, *Les Chevaliers de la Table Ronde*

The French poet and playwright Jean Cocteau (1889–1963) seems an unlikely writer to be attracted by the Arthurian legend, but his play Les Chevaliers de la Table Ronde *demonstrates just how seductive the subject has proved. Cocteau keeps the basic outline of the story, and its principal characters, but subverts the legend by emphasizing the role of Merlin, whom he portrays as a malevolent figure determined to undermine the Grail quest, and by creating a new character, Ginnifer, the mischief-making sprite in the magician's thrall, capable of changing shape at will and sowing discord at Arthur's court. The following scene opposes the 'true' Galahad and the 'false' Grail that exerts a seductive power over Arthur's knights and ultimately brings about the ruin of the Arthurian world.*

Artus – Knight, a miracle has brought you to our shores. A stone trough carried you over the waters. If this seat is yours, peace be with you. Alas, our table is empty indeed, since the princes who sat here are riding across the countryside in search of high adventure. Shall I name them for you?

Galahad – Sire, will you permit me?

Artus – Do you know their names?

Galahad – What knight searching for high adventure could fail to know Bohort, Perce-neige, Clamadieu, Florent of Itolac, King Beaudemagus, the seneschal Kay, Gamuret the Angevin and Patrice of the golden circlet? (*Rumblings*)

Artus – It is a marvel to hear you speak, fine sir. Allow me to present to you those who sit at this table and who wish to greet you. Lancelot of the Lake, the best knight in the world, son of the fairies, who was brought up by the same. Gawain, our nephew, who has a heart of gold and a head full of folly; our son Segramor, a poet who by some strange privilege has understood the language of birds since birth. He bears on his breast the bloody mark of the Perilous Seat. Standing, Merlin, our almoner and astrologer. And now, knight, and you my friends, I have a splendid surprise to announce to you. Beaudemagus, the magician king, who is kept, on account of his age, from travelling beyond his domain – from which no man returns – sends you in his place a speaking flower.

Galahad – …All that remains is for me to submit to the chair-test and then I shall seek out the castle of the Grail, Corbenic the undiscoverable.

Merlin – Knight, before you submit to the test, King Artus will read you the ritual. (*He bows*)

Artus (*standing, reads*) – Visible to some, invisible to others, a voluntary captive, the vessel of the Last Supper in which Joseph of Arimathea collected the blood of Christ awaits the Very Pure Knight at

Corbenic, a castle whose location is known to no man. (*Galahad kneels*) He who by his courage and wisdom succeeds in discovering the Grail, defeating the trickery that surrounds it, and passing through the mirages and phantoms; he who, being most attentive to certain signs, does not yield to tiredness or to the Ardour of asking many improper questions, but asks only a single one, will receive the reply: 'You are welcome and long awaited.' Then heavy things will become light and light things become heavy and the Grail will cease to be a mystery and the meaning of that which was obscure will be uncovered and spirit will rule over matter and dragons will perish and spread their tongues over the fable and truth will emerge straight as an arrow from its cocoon of idleness and enchantment. Galahad White-Armour, are you that man?

Galahad – I am.

Artus – Prove it.

Galahad – I will.

He walks round the table and sits down on the seat to the sound of trumpet blasts. He tears off his tunic and exposes his naked breast.

Jean Cocteau
Les Chevaliers de la Table Ronde, 1937

T. H. White

The British novelist T. H. White (1906–64) created a modern adaptation of the story, based on Malory's Morte d'Arthur *and written in a spirit that would have resonated with medieval readers. White's book is not a translation, but a reworking of the original which succeeds in giving new relevance to episodes that could easily have been disregarded as old-fashioned or obsolete. Applying the techniques of psychoanalysis to the description of traditional figures,*

White also shifts the chronology of events from the time of the Saxon invasions to the aftermath of the Norman Conquest: as a result the conflict is no longer between Britons and the Norman invaders, but between different sections of the Anglo-Norman population – a fact that gives the story a surprisingly modern twist. Finally, when Europe was beginning to feel the effects of the Nazi threat in 1941, White wrote a kind of prelude or epilogue to his Arthurian saga entitled The Book of Merlyn, *in which the disillusioned prophet-magician returns to his friends in the animal kingdom to reflect sadly on the risks and the responsibilities associated with political power. It was published in 1958 in* The Once and Future King, *a collection of the four novels.*

In The Sword in the Stone *Arthur, nicknamed the Wart, undergoes an unorthodox education at the hands of Merlin, who metamorphoses him into a variety of different animals in order to teach him to think like them, and not merely in the limited, arrogant manner typical of human beings. While all the knights are gathering in London for the election of the new King of England – who will prove his claim by freeing the sword from its bed of stone – Wart's adoptive brother, Kay, having forgotten his own sword, sends his half-brother in search of another. Arthur enters the church that contains the magic sword.*

'People,' cried the Wart. 'I must take this sword. It is not for me, but for Kay. I will bring it back.'

There was still no answer, and Wart turned back to the sword. He saw the golden letters on it, which he did not read, and the jewels on its pommel, flashing in the lovely light.

'Come sword,' said the Wart.

He took hold of the handles with both hands, and strained against the stone. There was a melodious consort on the recorders, but nothing moved.

The Wart let go of the handles, when they were beginning to bite into the palms of his hands, and stepped back from the anvil, seeing stars.

'It is well fixed,' said the Wart.

He took hold of it again and pulled with all his might. The music played more and more excitedly, and the lights all about the churchyard glowed like amethysts; but the sword still stuck.

'Oh, Merlyn,' cried the Wart, 'help me to get this sword.'

There was a kind of rushing noise, and a long chord played along with it. All round the churchyard there were hundreds of old friends. They rose over the church wall all together, like the Punch and Judy ghosts of remembered days, and there were otters and nightingales and vulgar crows and hares and serpents and falcons and fishes and goats and dogs and dainty unicorns and newts and solitary wasps and goat-moth caterpillars and corkindrills and volcanoes and mighty trees and patient stones. They loomed round the church wall, the lovers and helpers of the Wart, and they all spoke solemnly in turn. Some of them had come from the banners in the church, where they were painted in heraldry, some from the waters and the sky and the fields about, but all, down to the smallest shrew

mouse, had come to help on account of love. Wart felt his power grow.

'Remember my biceps,' said the Oak, 'which can stretch out horizontally against Gravity, when all the other trees go up or down.'

'Put your back into it,' said a Luce (or pike) off one of the heraldic banners, 'like you did once when I was going to snap you up. Remember that all power springs from the nape of the neck.'

'What about those forearms,' asked a Badger gravely, 'that are held together by a chest? Come along, my dear embryo, and find your tool.'

A Merlin sitting on the top of the yew tree cried out, 'Now then, Captain Wart, what is the first law of the foot? I thought I once heard something about never letting go?'

'Don't work like a stalling woodpecker,' urged a Tawny Owl affectionately. 'Keep up a steady effort, my duck, and you will have it yet.'

'Cohere,' said a Stone in the church wall.

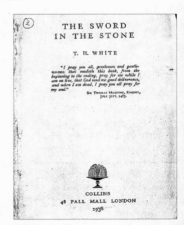

T itle page and (previous page) illustration from T. H. White's *Sword in the Stone*.

A snake, slipping easily along the coping which bounded the holy earth, said, 'Now then, Wart, if you were once able to walk with three hundred ribs at once, surely you can co-ordinate a few little muscles here and there? Make everything work together, as you have been learning to do ever since God let the amphibia crawl out of the sea. Fold your powers together, with the spirit of your mind, and it will come out like butter. Come along, homo sapiens, for all we humble friends of yours are waiting to cheer.'

The Wart walked up to the great sword for the third time. He put out his right hand softly and drew it out as gently as from a scabbard.

T. H. White
The Sword in the Stone, 1938

A tradition

White's book soon came to be regarded as a classic and became part of the school syllabus. A number of other writers took their cue from White, including the American novelist John Steinbeck (1902–68), whose Acts of King Arthur and his Noble Knights *is supposedly derived directly from the medieval texts. In other instances it is the structure rather than the details of the original that are re-used, as, for example, in* The Lyre of Orpheus *by the Canadian Robertson Davies, where the love triangle Arthur-Guinevere-Lancelot (most probably Gawain in the original) reappears in a modern form and receives a light-hearted, ironic treatment, turning the Arthurian myth into pastiche.*

Arthur's reign has begun; the king is married; the Saxons and the rebel barons have been subdued: what are Arthur and his knights to do now?

After a long and turbulent time, King Arthur, through fortune and force of arms, destroyed or made peace with his enemies inside his realm and out, and established in men's minds his right to rule. To accomplish this, the king had drawn to his person and his court the best knights and the hardiest fighting men in the world.

Having made peace through war, King Arthur found the dilemma of all soldiers in tranquillity. He could not disband his knights in a world where violence slept uneasily. And, on the other hand, it is difficult, if not impossible, to keep the strength and temper of fighting men without fighting, for nothing rusts so quickly as an unused sword or an idle soldier.

Arthur, knowing this, took the way of all generals in all time. He set up games which imitated war to keep his knights hard and hardy – jousts, tournaments, hunting, and endless warlike images. By these deadly games the fellowship of the Round Table sought to keep skill and courage high by venturing their lives in return for fame. In these games of simulated battle some knights increased in honor, while others were thrust down through misfortunate encounters with spear and sword on the tourney ground.

And while the older war-bred knights kept their arms bright, perhaps in memory of real battle, the young men, whose knighthood knew only the games of combat, did not love them.

Then Arthur learned, as all leaders are astonished to learn, that peace, not war, is the destroyer of men; tranquillity rather than danger is the mother of cowardice, and not need but plenty brings apprehension and unease. Finally he found that the longed-for peace, so bitterly achieved, created more bitterness than ever did the anguish of achieving it. King Arthur watched in apprehension while the young knights, who should have filled the fighting ranks, dissipated their strength in the mires of complaint, confusion, and self-pity, condemning the old time without having created a new one.

John Steinbeck
The Acts of King Arthur and his Noble Knights, 1976

Arthur and the heroic fantasy novel

Literary interest in the Arthurian legend has since extended to a relatively new genre of writing – the heroic fantasy novel, whose adventures are situated in imaginary universes where magic takes the place of science and where conflicts are resolved using medieval weapons. The Middle Ages, or 'Dark Ages', provide the setting for all these worlds, which are either co-existent with our own or located in an indeterminate past, either on Earth or some other planet. Rather than faith-fully re-creating the Arthurian stories, heroic fantasies rewrite the legend in their own fashion. The best-known work of this type – and one that has been resoundingly successful – is Marion Bradley's Mists of Avalon *(1983), which tells the entire story from the moment of Uther's union with Igraine up to the death of the king and the passing of the Arthurian world. The story, which is told partly in the first person – as if it were a diary written by Morgaine (Morgan le Fay) – emphasizes the role of the female figures, and in particular the conflict between the Christian Gwenhwyfar (Guinevere) and the pagan Morgaine. The novel is heavily influenced by New Age theories, and ideas about magic, witchcraft and a return to nature, but nevertheless parades before us an impressive panorama that draws on and reorganizes the material of the original legend.*

Here Morgaine, Arthur's half-sister and priestess of Avalon, awaits the return of the newly invested king and their forthcoming union, whereby they will enact the pagan rites according to which the sovereign, as incarnation of the male principle, weds the Great Goddess – Earth.

She was drawn to the last notch of tension, a strung bow pregnant with the arrow of power that must be sped. She touched the Horned One, releasing the power, and as if it sped through them all, they were off, running like the wind down the hillside, racing as if the very spring tides bore them. Behind them, feeling the power leave her, Morgaine crumpled and lay silent on the earth, feeling its damp chill strike up through her body. But she was unaware, tranced in the Sight.

She lay as if lifeless, but a part of her went with them, raced with them, speeding down the hillside, racing with the men of the tribe, flooding after the Horned One. Barking cries, as if they were hounds, sped after them, and a part of her knew that the women were crying out, speeding on the chase....

Darkness, the inner life of the forest closing around them; silence, the silence of the deer.... Morgaine, aware now of the forest as life and the deer as the heart of the forest, cast her power and her blessing through and over the forest. A part of her lay on the sunlit hillside, tranced, exhausted, letting the life of the sun flood through her, body and blood and inner being, and a part of her ran with deer and men until both were one...blending into one...the surges of life that were the quiet deer in their thicket, the little does, smooth and slender, the life racing in them as it raced in her body, the surges of life that

THE MISTS OF AVALON

Marion Bradley

The enthralling epic of passion and timeless enchantment

ere the men, slipping silent and intent rough the shadows....

Somewhere in the forest she felt the ing Stag fling up his head, sniffing the ind, aware for the scent of an enemy, ne of his own, one of the alien tribe of fe...she did not know whether it was e four-footed King Stag or the two-gged one she had blessed, they were ne in the life of the Mother Earth, d their lot was in the hands of the oddess....

Lying motionless, her face pressed to the earth and the flooding sun urning her back, time crawling and cing by turns, Morgaine began to see and from very far off it seemed that e had seen this before, in vision, metime, somewhere, a very long time 30 – the tall, sinewy youth, gripping his nife, falling, falling among the deer, nong the slashing hooves – she knew e screamed aloud, and simultaneously hew that her cry had rung everywhere,

so that even the King Stag paused in mid charge, appalled, hearing the shriek. There was a moment when everything stopped, and in that terrible moment of silence she saw that he scrambled to his feet, panting, charging with his head down, swinging his antlers, locking head-on, as he swayed and struggled, wrestling the deer with his strong hands and young body...a knife slashed upward; blood spilled on the earth, and he was bleeding too, the Horned One, blood on his hands, blood from a long slash on his side, the blood spilling on the earth, sacrifice spilled to the Mother that life should feed on her blood...and then the blood of the King Stag went over him in a gush as his blade found the heart, and the men around him rushed in with their spears....

She saw him carried back, covered in the blood of his twin and rival, the King Stag. All around him the little dark men were slashing, putting the raw, warm hide over his shoulders. Back they came in triumph, fires rising in the gathering dusk, and when the women lifted Morgaine she saw without surprise that the sun was setting, and she staggered, as if she too had run all day with the hunt and the deer.

They crowned her again with the crimson of triumph. The Horned One was brought before her, bleeding, and she blessed him and marked his forehead with the blood of the deer. The head was taken with the antlers which would bring down the next King Stag; the antlers which the Horned One had worn this day, broken and splintered, were cast into the fire. Soon there was a smell of burning flesh and she wondered if it was the flesh of man or stag.

Marion Bradley
The Mists of Avalon, 1983

Joan Wolf, *The Road to Avalon*

The Arthurian legend seems to hold a particular appeal for women. Joan Wolf's original novel gives us a completely new slant on the relationship between Arthur, Morgan and Mordred (Modred). Arthur is passionately in love with Morgan, but cannot marry her because she is his aunt (not his half-sister, as in the original), and Mordred, their son, is living at court in order to train for his future role as Arthur's successor. Spurred on by Agravaine, Mordred exposes the adultery between the queen and Bedwyr, Lancelot's prototype in the English-language texts, and provokes an angry reaction from his father.

He had left Mordred to the last. This was the interview he was most dreading. The boy must be made to understand the consequences of what he had done.

It was not going to be pleasant.

Even though Mordred lived down at the school with the other princes, he still had his own bedroom in the palace and it was there that Arthur went next. The bedroom was in Arthur's private suite, only a few doors down from the reception room that held Agravaine. Arthur put his hand on the door latch. How in Hades had the boy allowed himself to be so manipulated by Agravaine? he thought. And pressed down on the latch.

Mordred was standing by the window with his back to the room, a slender, almost fragile-looking figure. He appeared to be watching the sky. Morgan was right, Arthur thought: he had been better off in Lothian. He closed the door behind him and spoke Mordred's name.

The boy by the window turned slowly to face him. Mordred's face was pinched and sallow-looking, his eyes smudged with unhappiness and fatigue. 'I'm sorry, Father,' he said miserably. 'I didn't believe him, you see. He was saying filthy things about the queen and Bedwyr, and I thought I would let him make a fool of himself and shut him up once and for all.' The thin, beautiful face looked utterly stricken. 'I never for a minute thought that he was right.'

Arthur ruthlessly stifled the pity he felt for his son. Mordred had to be made to understand what he had done. 'I know you didn't mean to cause such trouble, Mordred,' he said in a quiet, level voice, 'but you have put me in a damnable position. You must realize that.'

'How *could* they?' Mordred cried passionately. 'How could they do that to you? Betray you? Deceive you?'

The king walked slowly across the tiled floor. '*They* have not betrayed me,' he said. 'You have.'

Mordred's head jerked as if he had been struck in the face. 'Nor have they deceived me,' Arthur went on remorselessly. 'I have known about the queen and Bedwyr for years.'

Mordred's face was chalk white. 'I don't understand.'

They were standing with but three feet between them. 'How old are you?' his father asked.

'Seventeen.'

'Seventeen. When I was seventeen I was high king and had lost the only person in the world I loved. I have never told this to anyone, but I thought quite seriously about taking my life.' Mordred's grey eyes were clinging to his face with horrified attention. 'I did not because I had responsibilities that went beyond my own personal needs. It is not a privilege to be king, Mordred. It is a responsibility. No matter what may happen, you must always remember th

ou are a king. That always must take
·recedence over your private feelings.
)o you understand what I am telling
ou?'

'I…Yes.'

'You let Agravaine use you for his
·wn ends. You were thinking like a
:hild, not like a king.'

Mordred pushed the hair back off his
·orehead. Some colour had come back
1to his face and he stared at his father
vith a glimmer of defiance. 'Well, if to
·e king means that I can no longer allow
1yself to feel, then you must find a new
·andidate for the job. I can't do it.'

Arthur's reply was measured. 'I did
·ot say you cannot allow yourself to
·el. I said that you must not allow your
·eelings to influence your public acts.'

'Don't you *care* about what they have
·one?' It was said wildly, passionately.

'I just told you that when I was your
·ge I lost the only person I ever loved.'
·rthur was watching him with an odd,
·lert look in his eyes. 'After ten long
·ears I got her back again. Why do you
·nink I go to Avalon, Mordred?'

The blood was pounding in
·Aordred's ears. 'To…to see Morgan.'

'To see Morgan. Your mother. I have
·ot touched Gwenhwyfar in years. I
·ertainly never begrudged her the
·appiness she found with Bedwyr.'

This is not happening, Mordred
·nought. My father is not saying these
·nings to me.

Joan Wolf
The Road to Avalon, 1989

·ernard Cornwell, *The Winter King*

*·he narrator, Derfel, is on the verge
·f entering a hopeless battle against the
·ilurians, sworn enemies of the late
·Iigh King Uther, whose legitimate son
·nd heir, Mordred, is still an infant.
·1 this version of the story, Arthur is one
of many bastards of Uther's, who has
trained as a warrior and a lord of battles
in Brittany.*

And then the horn sounded.

The horn gave a clear, cold note like
none I had ever heard before. There was
a purity to that horn, a chill hard purity
like nothing else on all the earth. It
sounded once, it sounded twice, and the
second call was enough to give even the
naked men pause and make them turn
towards the east from where the sound
had come.

I looked too.

And I was dazzled. It was as though
a new bright sun had risen on that dying
day. The light slashed over the pastures,
blinding us, confusing us, but then the
light slid on and I saw it was merely the
reflection of the real sun glancing from
a shield polished bright as a mirror.
But that shield was held by such a
man as I had never seen before; a man
magnificent, a man lifted high on a
great horse and accompanied by other
such men; a horde of wondrous men,
plumed men, armoured men, men
sprung from the dreams of the Gods
to come to this murderous field, and
over the men's plumed heads there
floated a banner I would come to love
more than any banner on all God's
earth. It was the banner of the bear.

The horn sounded a third time,
and suddenly I knew I would live,
and I was weeping for joy and all our
spearmen were half crying and half
shouting and the earth was shuddering
with the hooves of those Godlike
men who were riding to our rescue.

For Arthur, at last, had come.

Bernard Cornwell
*The Winter King:
A Novel of Arthur*, 1995

In the footsteps of King Arthur

The Arthurian legend has left its imprint on the landscape of Britain – from Tintagel (Arthur's birthplace) to Carmarthen (Merlin's city), from Cadbury Castle (Camelot?) to Glastonbury.

Glastonbury tower.

Tintagel

A pilgrimage to the sites associated with King Arthur should begin with Tintagel where the future king is said to have been conceived through the union of Uther Pendragon (under the assumed guise of the Duke of Cornwall, with the help of Merlin's magic) and the duchess Igerne. Standing high above the sea at the furthest tip of the Cornish peninsula, Tintagel justifies its reputation as an impregnable fortress and gives credence to the legend of the 'castle fairy' who makes a brief appearance four times a year at the solstices and the equinoxes. From Tintagel visitors can make a detour via southern Wales and the town of Carmarthen (Caer Myrddin, 'Merlin's city'), which owes its names to Merlin, the 'prophet of the English', who made the Round Table and counselled Uther and later Arthur. On the return from Carmarthen it is worth visiting Monmouth, birthplace of Geoffrey of Monmouth, who wrote the *Historia regum Britanniae*, the work responsible for establishing the Arthurian legend as part of Britain's literary heritage.

Camelot

The identification of Camelot – the capital built by the young king after he left 'Caerlion' or London – poses great problems. One of the most likely sites is the ruined castle of Cadbury, where recent archaeological excavations have uncovered the remains of Roman and Briton fortifications dating from the latter half of the 5th century, when Arthur is thought to have reigned. The names of two nearby villages, Queen Camel and West Camel, may indeed confirm the identification. However, Cadbury Castle is not the

Site of Arthur and Guinevere's tomb at Glastonbury.

same plain was the setting for the two most important battles of the Arthurian age: the first, during which Pendragon lost his life, and the final battle which claimed the lives of both Arthur and Mordred. A memorable monument to that first battle exists in the shape of Stonehenge, said during the Middle Ages to have been built by Merlin in memory of Pendragon, Uther's brother, at the beginning of the latter's reign.

Further to the north west lies Amesbury, in whose abbey Queen Guinevere supposedly sought refuge (later becoming abbess there) while fleeing Modred's attentions and forestalling Arthur's anger.

only contender: other possible sites exist much further north, on the borders of Northumberland, where Merlin's teacher is said to have lived in a forest and written down the story of King Arthur dictated by Merlin.

The few identifiable sites that appear in the list of twelve battles provided by Nennius are located in this same region. Most notably, the last battle, during which the Arthur of the *Annales Cambriae* is said to have lost his life, took place at 'Camlann', which may perhaps be identified with Camboglanna, the largest Roman fort constructed at the western end of Hadrian's Wall.

Mount Badon

Mount Badon, site of the 'historical' Arthur's great victory against the Saxons, has been tentatively identified with Liddington Castle, north of Salisbury Plain. According to the 12th-century French romances, this

Glastonbury

The focus of any visit to the legendary sites should be Glastonbury, identified in the 12th century with the Celtic Avalon, where the fairies were thought to have taken the wounded Arthur after the last battle. The hill crowned with the ruins of an ancient tower, Glastonbury Tor, rises high above the site of the medieval abbey and remains to this day a magical setting. It was in the Benedictine abbey, which had been partially destroyed by fire and was suffering major financial difficulties, that, in 1190, the tomb of King Arthur, complete with a magnificent Latin inscription, was discovered, and alongside what were assumed to be the bones of the king the remains of a head of golden hair identified as Guinevere's. Nothing remains of this tomb (sadly!) but a rectangle of grass with a notice indicating the tomb's discovery by a monk adept, no doubt, in the art of furthering his monastery's fortunes.

Anne Berthelot

King Arthur in the cinema

The popularity of the Arthurian legend, particularly in the English-speaking world, has led to the production of numerous films, of varying quality. Even leaving aside such classic works as The Knights of the Round Table *and the spectacular musical comedy* Camelot — *for millions of Americans the ultimate treatment of the subject — there have been four relatively recent, and very different, films demonstrating the continuing appeal of the King Arthur legend.*

Scenes from *The Knights of the Round Table* (above) and *Camelot* (left).

Robert Bresson, *Lancelot du Lac*

Lancelot du Lac by the French director Robert Bresson (1907–) was released in 1974 and was categorized as an 'artistic, avant-garde' film. The action takes place right at the end of the Arthurian era, following the quest for the Holy Grail, at a time when Arthur's knights have lost their enthusiasm and their raison d'être and no longer have a clear idea of their destiny. The camera focuses repeatedly on empty scenes that serve as testimony to the decadence of the Arthurian world, and the acting is deliberately neutral and disconnected from the dialogue. The fighting between the protagonists gives rise to scenes of uncompromising brutality in which we see limbs being severed and blood flowing freely. And while it is the adulterous relationship between Lancelot and Guinevere that precipitates the catastrophe, the love between the

throughout is on the barbarism of the Arthurian era rather than on the reputation of its heroes. It is hard to imagine a tragic film demythologizing the legend more effectively.

Monty Python and the Holy Grail

Monty Python and the Holy Grail (1975) also demythologizes the legend, but this time through comedy. King Arthur and his knights are like children playing at being knights. While their valets trot behind them carrying their harnesses and bashing pebbles together to make the sound of horses' hooves, they traipse around the countryside searching for new recruits for their quest and meeting the common folk who live a life bogged down in mud and poverty. Each of the

two is now only a pale reflection of their former passion and they are more anxious to avoid than seek one another out. The final conflict between Arthur and Lancelot is shown from a highly pessimistic angle and the emphasis

Scenes from *Lancelot du Lac* (above) and *Monty Python and the Holy Grail* (below).

heroes' adventures is a parody of traditional scenes from the medieval romances. When they attack a monstrous creature in its lair, the monster turns out to be, not a fire-breathing dragon, but a dangerous white vampire-rabbit with red eyes which hurtles through the air, attaches itself to the knights' throats and bleeds them dry. They meet terrible knights who say 'Ni' and terrorize the population by threatening to utter this unbearable sound; and the tests of initiation supposedly leading to the Grail finally fizzle out when the hero is arrested by a police inspector inquiring into the murder of a 20th-century historian, struck with a lance while doing his field work.

Eric Rohmer, *Perceval le Gallois*

Eric Rohmer's *Perceval le Gallois* (1978) was radically different from anything the director had done before, and completely different in approach from the two iconoclastic works by Bresson and Monty Python. The film is inspired by the romance of the same title by Chrétien de Troyes and scrupulously

PERCEVAL
LE GALLOIS

Scenes from *Monty Python and the Holy Grail* (left) and *Perceval le Gallois* (above and opposite).

PERCEVAL LE GALLOIS Ⓖ

PERCEVAL LE GALLOIS Ⓖ

follows its model, to the point that the dialogues (which retain where possible the cadence of the medieval octosyllable) are in a barely modified medieval French. The sets are symbolic, reduced to a handful of emblems (trees made of metal and plastic, for example). The film script precisely follows the original, at least in its first section, representing the ignorant young Welshman's first encounter with a group of knights, his departure for Arthur's court and disappointment on meeting the king; his unorthodox 'dubbing', and the various adventures that gradually transform him from a country oaf into a gallant and courtly knight, and which culminate in his visit to the Grail castle. The second part of Chrétien's romance is dedicated to the adventures of Gawain and was never finished; Rohmer chose to conclude it with a filmed version of

the liturgy relating to Christ's Passion.

John Boorman, *Excalibur*

John Boorman's *Excalibur* (1981), by contrast, provides a complete, two-hour résumé of the Arthurian legend from the moment of Arthur's conception, with Merlin's assistance, to that of his death in the battle against Modred, Arthur's son by his half-sister, including an abridged, but intelligently integrated version of the Grail quest. This spectacular production, inspired by Malory's *Morte d'Arthur*, is based on a series of rather facile ideas and a transparent symbolism, but nevertheless provides an excellent introduction to the story of Arthur and the Knights of the Round Table, Merlin and Uther, Guinevere, Lancelot, Perceval, Morgan and Modred. It is an atmospheric film which succeeds – in a way that a disparate collection of stories could never do – in conveying genuine emotion and a sense of nostalgia.

Anne Berthelot

Scenes from John Boorman's *Excalibur*. Left: A knight attempts to draw the sword from the stone. Above: Arthur's marriage to Guinevere. Opposite above: Arthur and Lancelot. Below: Merlin and some knights.

FURTHER READING

MEDIEVAL TEXTS AND STUDIES

Chrétien de Troyes, *Arthurian Romances*, translated by William W. Kibler, 1991

Geoffrey of Monmouth, *The History of the Kings of Britain*, translated by Lewis Thorpe, 1966

Layamon, *Brut* in Wace and Layamon, *Arthurian Chronicles*, translated by Eugene Mason, 1912

Malory, Thomas, *Le Morte d'Arthur*, 1976

Marie de France, *Old World Love Stories*, translated by Eugene Mason, 1913

La Mort le roi Artu, edited by Norris J. Lacy and translated by J. Neale Carman, 1974

The Mystery of King Arthur, edited by Elizabeth Jenkins, 1975

The Romance of Arthur, edited by James J. Wilhelm and Laila Zamuelis Gross, 1984

Sir Gawain and the Green Knight, translated by Brian Stone, 1974

Spenser, Edmund, *The Faerie Queene*, edited by A. C. Hamilton, 1977

Topsfield, Leslie Thomas, *Chrétien de Troyes: A Study of the Arthurian Romances*, 1981

Wace, *Roman de Brut*, in *Arthurian Chronicles*, translated by Eugene Mason, 1912

MODERN CRITICISM

Arthurian Literature in the Middle Ages, edited by Roger Sherman Loomis, 1959

Ashe, Geoffrey, *King Arthur: The Dream of a Golden Age*, 1990

The New Arthurian Encyclopaedia, edited by Norris J. Lacy, 1991

MODERN TEXTS

Alfred, Lord Tennyson, *Idylls of the King*, 1869

Bradley, Marion Zimmer, *The Mists of Avalon*, 1983

Cocteau, Jean, *Les Chevaliers de la Table Ronde*, 1937

Cornwell, Bernard, *The Winter King*, 1995

Morris, William, *The Defence of Guinevere*, 1858

Robinson, E. A., *Lancelot*, 1920

Steinbeck, John, *The Acts of King Arthur and his Noble Knights*, 1976

Twain, Mark, *A Connecticut Yankee in King Arthur's Court*, 1889

White, T. H. *The Once and Future King*, 1958

Wolf, Joan, *The Road to Avalon*, 1989

LIST OF ILLUSTRATIONS

DOCUMENTS

Excalibur disappearing into the lake, an engraving by Aubrey Beardsley for Thomas Malory's *Morte d'Arthur*.

INDEX

ACKNOWLEDGMENTS

The author and publishers would like to thank Caroline Alexander, Alban Cerisier, Nicole Loreau, Hugues Pradier and the Smithsonian Review.

PHOTO CREDITS

TEXT CREDITS

Grateful acknowledgment is made for use of material from the following works: pp. 140–1) Approximately 730 words from Marion Bradley, *The Mists of Avalon* (Michael Joseph), 1983; copyright © 1982 by Marion Bradley. Reprinted by permission of the author and the author's agents, Scovil Chichak Galen Literary Agency, Inc., New York. Reproduced by permission of Penguin Books Ltd. (pp. 117–8, 118–9) Approximately 1390 words from Chrétien de Troyes, *Arthurian Romances*, translated by William W. Kibler (Penguin Classics), 1991; copyright © William W. Kibler 1991; reproduced by permission of Penguin Books Ltd. (pp. 139–40) John Steinbeck, *The Acts of King Arthur and his Noble Knights* (William Heinemann), 1976; copyright © 1976 by the Estate of John Steinbeck; reprinted by permission of Random House UK Limited. (pp. 138–9) T. H. White, *The Sword in the Stone* (HarperCollins), 1938; reproduced by permission of David Higham Associates Limited. (pp. 142–3) From *The Road to Avalon* by Joan Wolf. Copyright © Joan Wolf, 1989. Reprinted by arrangement with Dutton Signet, a division of Penguin Books USA, Inc., and HarperCollins Publishers Ltd.

Anne Berthelot
is Professor of Medieval French Literature
at the University of Connecticut.
A specialist in the great prose romances of the
13th century, she is particularly interested
in the problems of enunciation and has written
a number of books and articles on the subject,
including *Figures et fonction de l'écrivain au
XIIIe siècle*. She is currently helping to edit the
Lancelot-Graal and is preparing a study of Merlin
in the literature of England, France and Germany
from the 12th to the 15th centuries.

Translated from the French by Ruth Sharman

For Harry N. Abrams, Inc.
Editor: Eve Sinaiko
Cover designer: Dana Sloan

Library of Congress Cataloging-in-Publication Data

Berthelot, Anne.
    [Arthur et la Table ronde. English]
    King Arthur and the knights of the Round Table / Anne Berthelot.
        p.   cm. — (Discoveries)
    Translated from the French original: Arthur et la Table ronde: La
force d'une légende.
    Includes bibliographical references and index.
    ISBN 0–8109–2887–6 (pbk.)
    1. Arthurian romances—History and criticism.   I. Title.
II. Series: Discoveries (New York, N.Y.)
PN685.B4713 1997
809'.93351—dc21   97–21474

Copyright © 1996 Gallimard

English translation copyright © 1997 Thames and Hudson Ltd., London

Published in 1997 by Harry N. Abrams, Inc., New York

Printed and bound in Italy by Editoriale Lloyd , Trieste